LIVING TRUSTS

and Simple Ways to Avoid Probate

LIVING TRUSTS

and Simple Ways to Avoid Probate

with forms

———

Karen Ann Rolcik

Attorney at Law

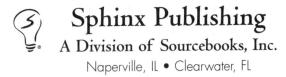

Sphinx Publishing

A Division of Sourcebooks, Inc.

Naperville, IL • Clearwater, FL

Second edition, 1998

Published by: **Sphinx® Publishing, A Division of Sourcebooks, Inc.®**

<u>Naperville Office</u>
P.O. Box 372
Naperville, Illinois 60566
(630) 961-3900
FAX: 630-961-2168

<u>Clearwater Office</u>
P.O. Box 25
Clearwater, Florida 33757
(727) 587-0999
FAX: 727-586-5088

Interior Design and Production: Shannon E. Harrington, Sourcebooks, Inc.

This publication is designed to provide accurate and authoritative information in regard to the subject matter covered. It is sold with the understanding that the publisher is not engaged in rendering legal, accounting, or other professional service. If legal advice or other expert assistance is required, the services of a competent professional person should be sought.

From a Declaration of Principles Jointly Adopted by a Committee of the
American Bar Association and a Committee of Publishers and Associations

Library of Congress Cataloging-in-Publication Data
Rolcik, Karen Ann.
    Living trusts, and simple ways to avoid probate : with forms /
Karen Ann Rolcik.—2nd ed.
        p.   cm.
Includes index.
    ISBN 1-57071-336-7 (pbk.)
    1. Living trusts—United States—Popular works.   2. Probate law
and practice—United States—Popular works.   3. Estate planning—
United States—Popular works.   I. Title.
KF734.Z9R65   1998
346.7305'2—dc21
                                                                    97-45084
                                                                       CIP

Printed and bound in the United States of America.

Paperback — 10 9 8 7 6 5 4 3

c.004

CONTENTS

Using Self-Help Law Books

Whenever you shop for a product or service, you encounter various levels of quality and price. In deciding what product or service to buy, you make a cost/value analysis on the basis of your willingness to pay and the quality you desire.

When buying a car, you decide whether you want transportation, comfort, status, or sex appeal. Accordingly, you decide among such choices as a Neon, a Lincoln, a Rolls Royce, or a Porsche. Before making a decision, you usually weigh the merits of each option against the cost.

When you get a headache, you can take a pain reliever (such as aspirin) or visit a medical specialist for a neurological examination. Given this choice, most people, of course, take a pain reliever, since it costs only pennies, whereas a medical examination costs hundreds of dollars and takes a lot of time. This is usually a logical choice because rarely is anything more than a pain reliever needed for a headache. But in some cases, a headache may indicate a brain tumor, and failing to see a specialist right away can result in complications. Should everyone with a headache go to a specialist? Of course not, but people treating their own illnesses must realize that they are betting on the basis of their cost/value analysis of the situation, they are taking the most logical option.

The same cost/value analysis must be made in deciding to do one's own legal work. Many legal situations are very straight forward, requiring a simple form and no complicated analysis. Anyone with a little intelligence and a book of instructions can handle the matter without outside help.

But there is always the chance that complications are involved that only an attorney would notice. To simplify the law into a book like this, several legal cases often must be condensed into a single sentence or paragraph. Otherwise, the book would be several hundred pages long and too complicated for most people. However, this simplification necessarily leaves out many details and nuances that would apply to special or unusual situations. Also, there are many ways to interpret most legal questions. Your case may come before a judge who disagrees with the analysis of our authors.

Therefore, in deciding to use a self-help law book and to do your own legal work, you must realize that you are making a cost/value analysis and deciding that the chance your case will not turn out to your satisfaction is outweighed by the money you will save in doing it yourself. Most people handling their own simple legal matters never have a problem, but occasionally people find that it ended up costing them more to have an attorney straighten out the situation than it would have if they had hired an attorney in the beginning. Keep this in mind while handling your case, and be sure to consult an attorney if you feel you might need further guidance.

Introduction

During the past twenty years, "how to avoid probate" has become the subject of countless speeches, books and seminars. The costs and time delays of probate and the court system have caused many people (including attorneys) to look for alternatives to the probate process.

Today there are a variety of probate alternatives available. Among these are life insurance contracts, pay on death accounts, joint tenancies, retirement accounts and various types of trusts. For many people, these methods may be used to completely avoid probate without any complications. These probate alternatives are discussed in greater detail in chapter 2.

The most popular probate alternative is the *living trust*. The living trust is a very effective method to avoid the probate process not only after a person's death but also during a person's life, in the event the person becomes incapacitated. The living trust is explained more fully in chapters 3 through 5.

The purpose of this book is to acquaint you with the various probate alternatives and to show you which ones will work best for your estate. A special emphasis is placed on the living trust because it has always been popular. However, you may learn from this book that simpler methods are available. If you do need a living trust, several basic forms are included to help you create your own. You should keep in mind that each of the probate alternatives discussed can be used in conjunction with one or more of the others. For example, you can use the beneficiary designation on your Individual Retirement Account (IRA) to transfer any assets remaining in your IRA at your death directly to your beneficiaries without making them pass through the probate process. The living trust can be used to transfer your other assets to your beneficiaries without making them pass through the probate process.

As the value of your estate increases the issues that must be considered change. Under the current federal estate tax (death tax) law, there is no tax payable to the Internal Revenue Service on the first $625,000 of property owned by a decedent (including life insurance and retirement accounts) at the date of his or her death. This amount is called the *unified credit* and is scheduled to rise to $1,000,000 by the year 2006. (This is discussed in greater detail in chapter 3.) If the value of your estate or the combined value of your estate and your spouse's estate exceeds the unified credit and you wish to avoid estate taxes, then you should consult a professional with experience in estate tax planning, generally a CPA or tax/estate planning attorney. Such a professional can give you advice concerning the proper way to structure your estate in order to take full advantage of the tax laws and reduce or eliminate estate taxes at your death. The forms included in this book are not intended for use by individuals or couples with estates over the unified credit who wish to avoid estate taxes. Additionally, if you own assets of an unusual character such as royalty interests, partnership interests or interests in trusts or annuities, or if there are complicated beneficiary distributions or conditions you wish to include in your living trust, you should consult an experienced professional. In many communities, living trusts are available for reasonable prices. No book of this type can cover every contingency in every case, but a knowledge of the basics will help you to make the right decisions regarding your property.

Do You Need an Attorney?

One of the first questions you will want to consider, and most likely the reason you are reading this book is: How much will an attorney cost? When billing on an hourly basis, estate planning attorneys will charge anywhere from $75 to $300 per hour. Many attorneys, however, have set fees for living trusts and these may range from $400 to $2,000 or more.

There are some advantages to hiring a lawyer. First, an attorney will be familiar with all of the state laws regarding trusts and this will save you the time of finding out if your state has peculiar rules governing trusts. Second, an attorney will be familiar with the most recent federal and state estate tax rules.

The primary advantage to creating your own living trust is that you can save money and can be certain that your living trust is completed when you are ready. Many lawyers have heavy workloads which can often result in matters being delayed for various periods of time. If you are creating your own living trust, you can do it at your own pace. Selecting an attorney is not easy. As the next section shows, it is hard to know whether you are selecting an attorney you will be happy with.

An alternative is to find an attorney who will be willing to accept an hourly fee to answer your questions and to give you help as you need it. This way you can save some legal costs but still get professional assistance.

Selecting an Attorney

A common, and frequently the best, way to find an attorney is to ask friends or acquaintances to recommend an attorney to you. You can also contact a lawyer referral service. This is a service that is usually operated by a local bar association and which is designed to match a client with a lawyer who actively handles cases in the area of law that the client needs. Lawyer referral services are usually listed in the yellow pages under "Attorneys."

You may also simply look under "Attorneys" in the yellow pages. Many lawyers list their areas of practice in their ads and some yellow pages list attorneys under various subheadings such as estate planning, wills, probate, personal injury, tax, etc.

However you find an attorney, you should have a clear understanding with the attorney regarding the amount of the fee, how the fee will be calculated, and exactly what will be done for the fee. For instance, does the attorney charge a set fee and if so what does that set fee include? Is there anything you will need that is not included in the fee, such as transferring your property to the trust? If the attorney charges on an hourly basis, find out how much the hourly rate is and how many hours the attorney estimates will be required to complete the matter. The fee understanding should be reached *before* you actually hire the lawyer.

THE PROBATE PROCESS

1

WHAT IS PROBATE?

Probate is the legal process by which property in an estate is transferred to the heirs and beneficiaries of a deceased person (the *decedent*). Heirs are persons who are entitled to receive a decedent's property if the decedent died without a will. Beneficiaries are persons who are named in a decedent's will to receive property.

The probate process begins by presenting to the judge the will of the decedent or, if there is no will, by presenting to the judge a list of the decedent's property and a list of the people to whom it is proposed that the property be given.

Generally, although each state will differ in the specific steps involved in the probate of a will, the following is a fairly representative outline of the probate process:

☛ A *petition* or *application* is filed with the probate court either asking that a will be admitted to probate, or stating that a person died without leaving a will.

☛ If there is a will, an order is signed admitting it to probate, and some type of document is issued by the court giving the personal representative power to act for the estate. This may be called

Letters of Administration, Letters Testamentary, Letters of Authority, or something similar. This may be done with or without a hearing, depending on the state and county.

☞ The executor must meet the qualifications of the state statutes setting forth who the state believes is competent to serve as executor.

☞ Unless the court grants special permission, the executor must post a surety bond.

☞ Notice of death is published or sent to the heirs and beneficiaries.

☞ A notice is sent to creditors to permit them time to file claims against the estate.

☞ The executor must collect all of the assets.

☞ Assets may be appraised to obtain a current value.

☞ An inventory must be prepared and filed with the court.

☞ The executor must pay the debts of the decedent and the expenses of the estate administration, including accountant and appraiser fees, probate costs, and the like.

☞ Assets are sold to raise cash to pay debts and expenses, if necessary.

☞ A final income tax return for the decedent must be filed. If there is more than $600 income during administration of the estate, the estate must file an income tax return and, if the estate is over $625,000 (rising to $1,000,000 in 2006), it must file an estate tax return. In some states, state income and estate tax returns must be filed.

☞ An accounting of the estate assets and the expenses of the estate must be filed with the probate court and approved.

☞ On petition, the probate court will close the administration of the estate.

☞ Executor and attorney's fees are paid.

☞ Assets are distributed to heirs or beneficiaries.

WHEN IS PROBATE NECESSARY?

Probate may be necessary whether or not a decedent had a will. A will does not eliminate the need for probate. The will is the primary document used in the probate process. Probate is required if the decedent owned property in his or her individual name at the time of his or her death.

If a decedent died without having signed a will, then the decedent died *intestate* and his or her property will pass to his or her *heirs at law*. The probate code of each state lists the heirs of a decedent, the order in which they will inherit from the decedent, and the amount of that inheritance. In effect, the state has written a will for the decedent and dictates who will receive the property without regard to the wishes of the decedent or the true needs of the decedent's family situation. If no living relative of the decedent can be located all of the decedent's property *escheats* to the state. That is, the state is the beneficiary of the decedent's entire estate!

If a decedent died with a signed will, then the decedent died *testate* and his or her property passes to the individuals named in his or her will, his or her beneficiaries. If a person challenges the validity of the decedent's will, often called *contesting the will*, the probate court will get involved in determining whether the beneficiaries named in the decedent's will are legally entitled to receive the property.

WHAT PROPERTY IS SUBJECT TO PROBATE?

Not all property owned by a decedent at the time of his or her death has to go through the probate process. Only *probate property* (also called *probatable assets*) is subject to the probate process. Probate property includes property owned in the individual name of the decedent alone or in the individual name of the decedent and another person without survivorship rights. Common examples of probate property are: bank accounts, securities, and other assets in the decedent's name alone; tangible personal property (e.g., jewelry, stamp collections, furniture, car); and real estate. If a husband and wife owned property jointly as *tenants by the entireties*, or if two people owned property as *joint tenants with rights of survivorship*, the property passes automatically to the survivor and does not go through the probate process. A certified copy of the decedent's death certificate generally is all that is required to show that the entire property interest in such accounts is held by the survivor.

Chapter 2 explains how to set up ownership of your property so that it is non-probate property and passes automatically upon your death.

THE ROLE OF YOUR WILL IN THE PROBATE PROCESS

A will allows you to decide who gets your property after your death. You can give specific gifts of personal items to certain persons and decide which of your friends or relatives deserve a greater share of your estate. You can also leave gifts to churches, schools and charities.

A will allows you to decide who will be the executor of your estate. Some states call the person who represents your estate and handles the probate process the *personal representative*. This is the same as an executor. An executor is the person who gathers together all of your assets and distributes them to the beneficiaries. With a will, you can provide that your executor does not have to post a surety bond with the court in order to serve which can save the estate money. The executor can also be granted broad powers in addition to the powers given to executors by law to handle estate matters.

A will allows you to choose a guardian for your minor children. This way, you can avoid fights among relatives and make sure that the person who is most familiar with you and your children raises your children. You may also appoint separate guardians over your children and over their money. For example, you may appoint your sister as guardian over your children and your father as guardian over their money. Thus, a second person could keep an eye on how your children's money is being spent.

DISADVANTAGES OF PROBATE

There are many disadvantages to the probate process. Each item discussed below is a good reason for trying to reduce your estate's exposure to probate. When all of the items are looked at together, the importance of reducing exposure to probate is unquestioned.

COSTS OF PROBATE

The costs of probate can be very significant. The size of your estate can be reduced, and you can lose large amounts of property you worked a lifetime to save. The costs of probate include filing fees, appraisers' fees, executor's fees, and attorney's fees. Each state has its own method by which probate attorneys can determine their fees for probate matters. Probate attorneys' fees may be calculated on an hourly basis, on a specific percentage of the value of the probate assets, or a combination of the two. Under any method, attorney fees for probate can be very significant.

TIME CONSUMING

The probate process is very time consuming and can cause long delays in transferring assets to your beneficiaries. Generally, the minimum period required to complete the probate process is four months. It is not unusual for the typical probate to take as many as eighteen months. Many probates can take as long as two or even five years! During this time, money is tied up and possibly household expenses (other than the bare necessities) and college tuitions can be interrupted until the probate is completed. It may be possible to get some of the assets released prior to the completion of the probate by asking special permission from the probate court. However, this may cost additional money for attorney fees and will generally require a showing of need. This all becomes part of the public record and can at times be embarrassing for the surviving family members.

LACK OF
PRIVACY

Once your will is admitted to probate it becomes a matter of public record. Anyone in the world can go to the courthouse and look at your will. Although some states seal the inventory of the estate, generally the identity of your beneficiaries and the inventory of your assets, including their value, are available for inspection by anyone who asks. It is not uncommon for financial advisors, insurance agents, estate liquidators and the like to look up estate values in the courthouse and contact the family offering services and to "assist" the family in their time of need.

LACK OF
CONTROL

A will can be subject to challenge by disgruntled heirs. This can undermine the power of the executor over the distribution of your assets and the implementation of your wishes until the will contest is resolved by the probate court.

ADVANTAGES OF PROBATE

Despite the problems of probate described above there are several reasons why in some cases probate should not be avoided *entirely*. While many people will not view these reasons as "advantages" to probate, there are benefits that can be gained from probate.

GUARDIANS FOR
MINOR
CHILDREN

First, generally only a will can name guardians to take care of your minor children. The probate court will almost always honor a designation of guardian in a will. Only in those rare circumstances that the court finds evidence that the person named in the will is not suitable to take care of and raise your children, will the court appoint someone else who it believes is better qualified. If you have minor children you should have a will which names a guardian, and the will will need to be admitted to probate. However, you do not have to have any of your assets go through probate.

LIMITING CREDITOR CLAIMS

Second, after the will is admitted to probate the executor will be required to give notice to any creditor you may have at the time of your death. Often this notice is published in a newspaper. As soon as the notice is given, the clock starts ticking and the creditors only have a limited period of time during which to contact the executor and formally file a claim for payment against the estate.

If the creditor does not file the claim within the prescribed time period, its claim is cut off in the future. This time period is called the *statute of limitations*—a statute that limits the amount of time the creditor has to file its claim. If you have only limited, known debts this may not be a problem, but if there are any potential claims against your estate, such as from a business venture, heirs you left out of your will, or unpaid taxes, you may wish to have a probate filed at your death to cut off those claims. Even if only $100 is subject to probate, your will can invoke the protections of the probate system such as starting the statute of limitations.

TRANSFER OF ALL ASSETS

Finally, if probate alternatives are used, including the living trust, there may be some assets that do not get transferred to the trust or that are not covered by a beneficiary designation. Such assets may include last minute inheritances, lawsuit awards, etc. Your will makes certain that such property goes to the beneficiaries you designate and does not pass pursuant to the "will" that the state writes for you if you die intestate.

It is not necessary to write a will that names the beneficiaries of the probate assets. Instead, a *pour over will* can be used. A pour over will picks up the assets outside of the living trust, through the probate process, and "pours" them over into your living trust to be administered and distributed according to the terms of the trust. Once again, this ensures the privacy of the distribution of your assets. Forms 1 and 2 are examples of pour over wills. Because each state has different rules regarding the appointment of executors, guardians, and the like, it is important to consult an attorney or a self-help law book that specifically deals with the requirement for wills in your state.

For these reasons, not everyone would be advised to avoid probate completely. Instead, you should take advantage of every alternative available to minimize the contact your estate will have with the probate process, but have a will which can be probated in the event the above situations occur. The laws authorize these alternatives and you should take advantage of them to the greatest extent possible.

PROBATE ALTERNATIVES 2

There are several ways to keep your assets from going through the probate process after your death. These probate alternatives include various forms of joint tenancy, contractual dispositions of property, lifetime gifts, and the use of trusts. These alternatives are not mutually exclusive. You can use more than one at a time. In fact, it is often advisable to use several probate alternatives. It is very important, however, that you coordinate the use of the probate alternatives to make certain that your wishes are carried out.

For example, you may wish to make provisions in your living trust to ensure financial security not only for your spouse and children but also for your parents. However, if your life insurance and retirement plan beneficiary designations and joint bank accounts name your spouse as the sole beneficiary, your parents and perhaps your children will not receive the financial benefits of those assets. In such a case, it would be important to change those beneficiary designations to name your living trust as the primary beneficiary. The property will then be subject to the terms of the living trust and your intentions will not be thwarted. Funding your living trust will be discussed in detail in chapter 5.

There are many benefits of these probate alternatives. First, of course, is the ability to bypass the probate process and its costs and delays. Second, these alternatives are very flexible techniques. For example, bank accounts can be opened and closed easily and generally without cost to the account owner. Thus, if you want to change the joint tenant on an account you can simply go to the bank and change the account name and signature card. Third, these probate alternatives are generally very inexpensive to establish. Finally, the time and effort to implement these alternatives is relatively minimal compared to the time and expense of probate.

JOINT TENANCY

Joint tenancy is the easiest and most inexpensive way to avoid probate. A joint tenancy is created by the instrument giving title to the asset. Common examples of this type of instrument are deeds, stock certificates, and bank or brokerage accounts. Generally, three types of joint tenancy can be created, but only two avoid probate.

JOINT TENANTS WITH RIGHTS OF SURVIVORSHIP

The most popular form of joint tenancy is "joint tenants with rights of survivorship" (JTWROS). This form of joint tenancy can exist between any two or more individuals—it is not limited to husband and wife. Common JTWROS assets are real estate, bank or brokerage accounts, stocks, bonds, etc. The most common use of JTWROS are with regard to bank accounts and real estate.

During lifetime, each joint tenant has full rights of ownership with respect to only that portion of the property which he or she contributed to the account but has full access to all of the property. He or she can withdraw all of the funds even though he or she may have only contributed a minimal amount to the account. The financial institution is not required to determine whether he or she is withdrawing more than his or her contribution.

At death, a joint tenant's share automatically passes to the surviving tenant and is not subject to the probate process. However, when the surviving tenant later dies, the property is included in his or her probate estate and must go through the probate process prior to being distributed to the beneficiaries. Typically, a JTWROS designation is made by using the word "OR." For example, "Thomas or Roberta as joint tenants with rights of survivorship."

Example.

> Angie puts $10,000 into a bank account and names her son, Dave, as joint tenant with rights of survivorship. When Angie became sick and could not handle her financial affairs, Dave could pay her bills because he was one of the "owners" of the account. There was no need to go through the lengthy process of having David appointed guardian for Angie to handle her financial affairs. On Angie's death, the bank account passes to Dave automatically without going through the probate process. However, at Dave's later death, the assets will pass through the probate process unless he adds another joint tenant to the account.

You must be aware that a JTWROS account is risky. While it provides convenience during lifetime by giving another person access to the funds, that same convenience can cause problems. If you put your real estate into joint ownership with someone, you cannot sell it or mortgage it without that person's signature. If you put your bank account in joint ownership with someone, they can take some or all of the money in the account without your consent or knowledge. Also, if you put property in joint ownership with someone: 1) if they are married, their spouse may claim a portion of the property in a divorce, 2) if they get sued, the person getting a judgment may try to take the property to satisfy the judgment, and 3) if they file for bankruptcy, the bankruptcy trustee may try to bring the property into the bankruptcy proceedings.

Example 1.

> Alex put his bank accounts into joint ownership with his daughter Mary. Mary fell in love with Doug, who was in trouble with the law. Doug convinced Mary to "borrow" $30,000 from the account for a "business deal" that went sour. Later, she "borrowed" $25,000

more to pay Doug's bail bond. Alex didn't find out until it was too late that his money was gone.

Example 2.

Jane put her bank account into joint ownership with her son, Joe, who is married to Lisa. Two years later, Lisa files for divorce and claims the bank account as part of her marital property. Now Jan has to hire a lawyer to fight Lisa's claim.

If JTWROS is used (or an estate by the entireties, discussed below), it overrides a will and a living trust. Therefore, if you use tenancy by the entireties or JTWROS it is very important to make certain that the ownership of the account is consistent with your overall intentions. If you want all of your estate to go to your sister and make her the sole beneficiary of your will or living trust, don't put your assets into a joint account with your brother because they will automatically go to him without even going into your estate.

Example.

Bill's will leaves all of his property to his wife, Mary. Bill dies owning a house jointly with his sister, Ann, and a bank account jointly with his son, Don. Upon Bill's death Ann gets the house, Don gets the bank account and his wife Mary gets nothing.

Personal property and joint tenancy. While the issue of who owns personal property does not come up often, where the property is valuable you should take the necessary steps to be sure that it is titled as you wish. Property that is represented by a physical title, such as shares of stock, bank accounts and real estate, is easy to set up in joint tenancy, but personal property, such as furniture, coins or silverware is a little trickier. To make it clear what type of ownership such property is in, you need some sort of paper for your records. This can be the receipt you received from the store, or a bill of sale. For property you already own, you can transfer it to a third party, such as your sister, and have her transfer it back to you and your spouse, or your children clearly stating that is it owned in joint tenancy.

```
John Smith and Mary Smith, husband and wife, as joint
tenants with full rights of survivorship.
```

Forms 12 and 13 can be used to convert personal property you already own into JTWROS property as described above. Form 12 (Part A) transfers the property from you to another person (called a *strawman*), and Form 13 (Part B) transfers the property from the strawman to you and the other joint tenant.

The strawman can be anyone over the age of 18 (except the intended joint tenant), but you should be sure the person you use as the strawman does not have any judgments against him or her. Technical aspects of the law in many states require the use of the strawman and the two-part form.

To complete Form 12, (Part A):

1. Fill in the date where indicated at the top left of the form.

2. In the main paragraph, type in your name on the line for the "assignor." If you already hold the property with someone else, both names should go on this line. For example, if you and your spouse currently own the property, and you want to add your daughter's name, then both you and your spouse's names should be typed in.

3. In the main paragraph, type in the strawman's name on the line for the "assignee."

4. In the space after the main paragraph, type in a description of the property being transferred. Be as specific as possible in describing the property, including such things as the make, model, serial number, etc., if such information is available.

5. You (and any other assignors), and the assignee (strawman) need to sign where indicated at the bottom of the form.

To complete Form 12, (Part B):

1. Fill in the date where indicated at the top left of the form.

2. In the main paragraph, type in the strawman's name on the line for the "assignor."

3. In the main paragraph, type in your name, and the name (or names) of the person (or persons) you want to be joint owners with you.

4. In the space after the main paragraph, type in the same description of the property as you did in Form 12 (Part A).

5. Type in the names of the new joint owners in the paragraph after the space for the property description, then check the second box for "as joint tenants with full rights of survivorship." However, if you and your spouse are to hold the property as joint tenants (because your state does not permit tenancy by the entireties, check the third box for "Husband and Wife, as joint tenants with full rights of survivorship."

6. The assignor (strawman), and you and the other assignee (or assignees) need to sign where indicated at the bottom of the form.

Example.

John owns an antique roll-top desk in his own name (or with no written evidence as to ownership). He wants his daughter, Sally, to inherit it upon his death, without having to go through probate. John can convey the desk first to Mike (using Form 12), who will then reconvey it to John and Sally as JTWROS (using Form 13). When John dies, it automatically goes to Sally, without the need for probate.

Note. In Alaska only a husband and wife may hold real estate in joint tenancy, in Pennsylvania it is not clear whether real estate can be held in joint tenancy, and in Tennessee no property may be held in joint tenancy except by a husband and wife. In Texas property may be held by a husband and wife in joint tenancy if there is a written agreement signed by them that clearly describes the property and uses language such as: "husband and wife, as joint tenants with full rights of survivorship."

TENANCY BY
THE ENTIRETIES

A second type of joint tenancy is *tenants by the entireties*. This form of joint tenancy is similar to JTWROS but can only exist between a husband and wife and is not recognized in all states. Tenancy by the entireties for real estate is recognized in the following states: Alaska, Arkansas, Delaware, District of Columbia, Florida, Hawaii, Indiana, Maryland, Massachusetts, Michigan, Mississippi, Missouri, New Jersey, New York, North Carolina, Ohio, Oklahoma, Oregon, Pennsylvania, Rhode Island, Tennessee, Utah, Vermont, Virginia, and Wyoming. If tenancy by the entireties is not available in your state, you should review the previous section on joint tenancy.

Tenancy by the entireties historically served as a form of protection for the interests of spouses in real estate acquired during a marriage. It prevents a husband from selling or otherwise transferring real estate without his wife's knowledge or permission. Each spouse owns an equal share of the asset. Tenancy by the entireties can be dissolved by divorce, death, or sale of the asset. At the death of a spouse, his share passes automatically to the surviving spouse and is not subject to the probate process.

Example.

> Mike and Joan are married. During their marriage they purchase a home as tenants by the entireties. While they are alive both have the right to use the property. Neither can sell or give away his interest in the property without the other's permission. When Mike dies, his interest automatically passes to Joan. His will does not control the property and therefore, the property is not subject to probate.

Personal property and tenancy by the entireties. Tenancy by the entireties for personal property is recognized in the following states: Alaska, Arkansas, Delaware, District of Columbia, Florida, Hawaii,

Maryland, Massachusetts, Mississippi, Missouri, Ohio, Oklahoma, Oregon, Pennsylvania, Rhode Island, Tennessee, Utah, Vermont, Virginia, and Wyoming. When personal property is purchased, a receipt or bill of sale as described in the previous section on joint property should be used. You must make sure that your receipt or bill of sale lists you and your spouse as follows:

```
John Smith and Mary Smith, husband and wife,
in an estate by the entireties.
```

Once again, you can create a tenancy by the entireties for personal property you already own in the same manner as described in the previous section. Forms 12 and 13 can be used to accomplish this. You can complete the form by following the instructions in the previous section on joint property, with the following exceptions:

1. In Form 12, the assignees can only be you and your spouse.

2. In Form 13, you will check the box for "as husband and wife, in an estate by the entireties."

Example.

> Bob and Lauri are married. Bob owned personal property before they got married and now wants to make it property that he and Lauri own as tenants by the entireties. Bob can transfer the property to Jake who will then transfer it to Bob and Lauri as tenants by the entireties.

Two words of caution with regard to Forms 12 and 13 and the creation of JTWROS and tenancies by the entireties for personal property. First, there is no guarantee that Forms 12 and 13 will be effective in your state to create JTWROS or tenancies by the entireties for personal property. However, there is no disadvantage to using this form. It is always better to have documents to support your position and evidence of your intention to create a joint tenancy. Second, such transfers may be considered a gift, which may have tax consequences if the value of the property is great enough. Therefore, you may want to consult your tax adviser before making a transfer. For more information, see the section on OUTRIGHT GIFTS later in this chapter.

TENANCY IN
COMMON

The third form of joint tenancy is *tenancy in common*. A tenancy in common requires no less than two people to own the asset. Each person owns an equal share of the property and while alive each person can use the property. At the death of an owner, his or her share passes pursuant to his or her will, or if he or she has no will to his or her heirs at law. Tenants in common does not avoid the probate process.

Example.

> John and Mary aren't married but own a house as tenants in common. While they are alive both are entitled to use the property. John can sell or give away his interest in the property without Mary's permission. Consequently, Mary can become a tenant in common with a complete stranger. When John dies, his half ownership interest in the house passes to the beneficiaries named in his will. Those beneficiaries now are tenants in common with Mary. Mary still owns her share.

COMMUNITY PROPERTY

Only eight states recognize this method of asset ownership: Arizona, California, Idaho, Louisiana, Nevada, New Mexico, Texas and Washington. However, Wisconsin's system is nearly identical to community property. This is a special type of ownership that exists only between a husband and wife. Special state laws govern and protect the rights of a spouse in property acquired during the marriage. Generally, similar to a tenancy by the entireties, a spouse owns only one-half of the property and cannot sell, transfer or encumber the property without the other spouse's permission. Community property status attaches to most property acquired during the marriage. If you live in a community property state you can still pass property to a person other than your spouse at your death but you can only give one-half of it away.

TRANSFERS OF PROPERTY BY CONTRACT

Some types of property avoid the probate process through the "contract" that establishes the ownership and ownership rights of the property. The "contract" sets forth the rules governing how the property may be used during your lifetime and how it will be disposed of at your death. You name the beneficiary of the property, the person who will receive it at your death, and the other party must comply with the terms of the contract and distribute the property to that person after your death. Because the property is subject to a private contract, it is not subject to the probate process.

Two common examples of this are, annuities and stock option contracts.

PAY ON DEATH BANK ACCOUNTS

Financial institutions will allow you to set up your account so that upon your death it will go to the person or persons you name as beneficiary. This is not a joint account; the beneficiary cannot get the money until you die. You retain complete control of the account during your life. Such an account may be called a POD (pay on death) account, a TOD (transfer on death) account, or an I/T/F (in trust for) account. Lawyers call them "Totten Trusts" after the party who first went to court to settle the issue that they are legal.

With a pay on death account you can change the beneficiary any time you want and the person who will receive the money upon your death does not need to know about it until your death.

Example.

> Michael opened a bank account in his name "I/T/F Judy." When Michael dies, the account automatically passes to Judy without going through probate. During his life, Michael has complete control over the account and can name someone other than Judy as

beneficiary simply by changing the title of the account. Judy cannot withdraw any funds during Michael's life.

PAY ON DEATH SECURITIES REGISTRATION

The drawback of pay on death accounts was that they could only be used for cash in a bank account. Anyone with stocks or bonds had to set up a living trust to keep them out of probate. But beginning in 1990 various states began passing a law allowing securities (stock, binds and mutual fund shares) to be registered in pay on death form. This change in the law will make avoiding probate easier for many more people.

Unfortunately, as of 1997, only twenty-seven states have passed this new law. But in a few years it will probably be accepted throughout the country.

The states that allow transfer on death as of publication of this book are listed in the following table, along with the reference to the relevant state statute. If your state is not listed you should call your broker or mutual fund agent to see if the law in your state has changed recently.

Alabama	Code 1975, §§ 8-6-140 to 8-6-151
Alaska	A.S. §§ 13.06.050; 13.33.301 to 13.33.310
Arizona	A.R.S. §§ 14-1201; 14-6301 to 14-6311
Arkansas	A.C.A. §§ 28-14-101 to 28-14-112
Colorado	C.R.S.A. §§ 15-10-201; 15-15-301 to 15-15-311
Delaware	12 D.C.A. §§ 801 to 812
Florida	F.S. §§ 711.50 to 711.512
Idaho	I.C. §§ 15-6-301 to 15-6-312
Illinois	S.H.A. 815 ILCS 10/0.01 to 10/12
Indiana	West's A.I.C. 32-4-1.6-1 to 32-4-1.6-15
Iowa	I.C.A. §§ 633.800 to 633.811
Kansas	K.S.A. §§ 17-49a 01 to 17-49a 12
Maryland	Maryland Code, Estates & Trusts, §§ 16-101 to 16-112
Michigan	M.C.L.A. §§ 451.471 to 451.481
Minnesota	M.S.A. §§ 542.1-201; 524.6-301 to 524.6-311
Mississippi	Code 1972, §§ 91-21-1 to 91-21-25

Montana	M.C.A. §§ 72-1-103; 72-6-301 to 72-6-311
Nebraska	R.S.N. §§ 30-2209; 30-2734 to 30-2746
Nevada	N.R.S. 111.480 to 111.650
New Hampshire	RSA 563-C:1 to 563-C12
New Jersey	N.J.S.A. § 3B:30-1 to 3B:30-12
New Mexico	N.M.S.A. §§ 45-1-201; 45-6-301 to 45-6-311
North Dakota	N.D.C.C. §§ 30.1-01-06; 30.1-31-21 to 30.1-31-30
Ohio	O.R.C. §§ 1709.01 to 1709.11
Oklahoma	71 O.S.A. §§ 901 to 913
Oregon	O.R.S. §§ 59.535 to 59.585
Pennsylvania	20 Pa.C.S.A. §§ 6401 to 6413
South Dakota	S.D.C.L. §§ 29A-6-301 to 29A-6-311
Utah	U.C.A. §§ 75-6-301 to 75-6-313
Virginia	C.V. §§ 64-1-206 to 64.1-206.8
Washington	R.C.W.A. §§ 21.35.005 to 21.35.901
West Virginia	W.V.C. §§ 36-10-1 to 36-10-12
Wisconsin	W.S.A. §§ 705.21 to 705.30
Wyoming	W.S.A. §§ 2-16-101 to 2-16-112

TRANSFER ON DEATH AUTOMOBILE REGISTRATION

At present only two states, California and Missouri, allow transfer on death automobile registration. However, in the next few years other states may pass similar laws. Check with your motor vehicle registration department to see if this type of registration is allowed in your state.

LAND TRUSTS

Although real estate cannot be registered in Transfer on Death form, and joint ownership may cause problems, land trusts are becoming popular in many states to accomplish the same thing.

A land trust is an arrangement where you put title to your property in the name of a trustee but you have all the rights and responsibilities for the property as if it were in your name. This type of trust is typically called an *Illinois-type* land trust, or a title-holding trust. Under such a trust the only thing the trustee does is hold title.

The trustee can be a bank, your attorney, a relative or even yourself. Some people set up a separate trust for each property they own. The terms of the trust provide that upon your death a named beneficiary becomes the owner of the trust and can immediately take charge of the property. Land trusts offer many benefits other than probate avoidance, such as keeping your name off the public records and keeping the purchase and sales price secret.

Currently not all states allow land trusts, but the American Bar Association is working on a law that can be passed in all states, so they may become more available soon. States that can clearly use land trusts today are listed below. Land trusts may be created in many other states if they are carefully worded. You should consult an attorney with experience in land trusts if you wish to use such a trust.

Arizona	Hawaii	North Dakota
Arkansas	Illinois	Ohio
Florida	Indiana	Virginia

LIFE INSURANCE

Another popular probate alternative is a life insurance policy. A life insurance policy is a contract between the owner of the policy and the life insurance company. Generally, the person who purchases the policy, the "owner," is also the person whose life is insured. When the policy is purchased the life insurance company will ask the owner to designate the beneficiary of the life insurance policy. The beneficiary is the person who will receive the money that the policy pays when the owner dies. The owner will name a beneficiary and this beneficiary designation becomes part of the life insurance contract.

As long as the owner pays the premiums on the policy, the life insurance company agrees to pay the proceeds of the policy to the beneficiary when the owner dies. Typically, when the owner dies, the life insurance company will require proof of death in the form of a death certificate, will require that a claim form be completed, and will automatically pay the policy proceeds directly to the beneficiary. This happens completely outside of the probate process. The cash is available to the beneficiary quickly which often will help a surviving spouse make mortgage payments, pay utility bills and pay college tuition bills. Unless the owner has designated his or her estate or the executor of his or her estate (in his or her capacity as executor) as beneficiary of the policy, the policy proceeds will not be subject to the probate process.

Example.

> Mark buys a life insurance policy from Life Company and designates Rebecca as beneficiary of the policy proceeds upon his death. As long as Mark continues to pay the premiums, at his death Life Company will be required to pay the proceeds to Rebecca when Mark dies. Since the life insurance policy provides that the proceeds are to be paid directly to Rebecca, they are not subject to the probate process. However, if Mark had named his estate as beneficiary, upon his death Life Company would pay the proceeds to his estate and the proceeds would be subject to the delays and costs of probate.

Often a parent or grandparent will name a minor child as beneficiary of a life insurance policy. Typically, the insurance companies will require that a legal guardianship be established for the minor before it pays the proceeds of the policy. Such a guardianship requires filing documents with the probate court which costs money and takes time. Under a guardianship for a minor, the guardian will be required to hold the policy proceeds for the minor and distribute them to the minor when he or she reaches age eighteen or twenty-one in some states. A living trust can provide that such life insurance proceeds be held for the child's benefit until beyond the age of eighteen or twenty-one.

Although the proceeds of a life insurance policy do not pass through probate, the value of the proceeds is included in the estate in determining if it is over $625,000 (rising to $1,000,000 by 2006) for estate tax purposes. One way to avoid this is if the policy is owned by a person other than the decedent. For example, if you wish to purchase a life insurance policy on yourself, you could instead give the money to your son and have him purchase the policy on you. That way he or she owns the policy and it is not part of your estate. Of course, if the money you gave your son is substantial you may have to pay a gift tax on it. However, this can be risky. As the owner of the policy, your son can change the beneficiary of the policy. Thus, if you intended that the policy be paid to all of your children equally, your son can change this, without your knowledge, to pay all of the policy proceeds to him.

As you can see, this area of law gets complicated and if you wish to use all the loopholes you should consult an expert in estate planning.

RETIREMENT PLANS

Individual Retirement Accounts (IRAs), company pension plans, profit-sharing plans, and 401(k) plans are very popular. Each of these "retirement plans" are funded with assets such as cash, stocks, bonds, mutual funds, etc. These retirement plans are essentially a specialized form of savings account subject to very strict tax rules. When a person retires or reaches a certain age (often sixty-two or sixty-five), he or she can begin to withdraw funds from the retirement plan. If the owner dies before receiving all of the funds in his or her retirement plan, a beneficiary designated by the owner will receive the funds remaining in the retirement plan. Just like the life insurance contract, the owner of the retirement plan will complete a beneficiary designation which will direct the employer, brokerage firm, or bank (if the retirement plan is an IRA bank account) to pay the funds to a specific individual (or individuals) upon the death of the owner.

The employer, brokerage firm, or bank is required to honor the contract and make the payment after the death of the owner.

Example.

> Kevin worked for USA Company and made contributions to a 401(k) retirement plan sponsored by the Company naming Glenda as beneficiary. Kevin retires and begins to receive payments each year from the plan. Kevin dies and $50,000 remains in the plan. USA Company must pay the $50,000 directly to Glenda without going through the probate process.

There are many very specialized tax rules governing who may be named beneficiary of a retirement plan. Some tax options are only available to a surviving spouse. If you are considering naming someone other than your spouse (including your living trust) as beneficiary of your retirement plans you should consult a professional with experience in this specialized tax area.

In addition to the transfers of property by joint tenancy or contract, there are two other commonly used methods to transfer property without going through the probate process—outright gifts and trusts.

OUTRIGHT GIFTS

Property can be transferred to your beneficiaries by means of an outright gift during your lifetime. Under the current federal gift tax law, an individual can give up to $10,000 a year, or a husband and wife can together give up to $20,000 a year, to any number of people, free of gift tax. (This $10,000 or $20,000 amount is often called the *annual exclusion gift*. The Taxpayers Relief Act of 1997 provides that it be indexed for inflation, so it will likely rise slightly over the years.) The person receiving the property must receive it with "no strings attached." The property becomes theirs subject to their complete control. The person receiving the property does not have to pay income tax on the property he or she receives.

Federal law also permits you to transfer up to $625,000 (rising to $1,000,000 by the year 2006) either during your lifetime or at your death free of federal estate or gift tax. Thus, in addition to the annual exclusion gift you can make gifts of up to this amount during your lifetime with no gift tax. However, if you give away more than this amount during your lifetime, then at your death every dollar that your beneficiaries receive is taxed and the rate starts at thirty-seven percent!

If you give any gifts in excess of the annual exclusion gift during a year, you are required to file a federal gift tax return even if no tax is due because you are using up your unified credit. This gift tax return is due on April 15 of the year following the year in which you make the gifts. A copy of the federal gift tax return, Form 709, is included in appendix B.

TRUSTS

For hundreds of years trusts have been the most popular way to avoid probate, especially for large estates. Today, with pay on death accounts and other devices described earlier, trusts may not be necessary for as many estates, but they can still provide advantages for many situations.

A trust is a legal "person" that comes into existence when an individual signs a legal document which contains certain provisions. A trust can be an *inter vivos* trust (meaning it is created during one's life) or a *testamentary* trust (meaning it does not start until one's death). It can be *revocable* (meaning it can be changed at any time) or *irrevocable* (meaning it can usually never be changed).

The person who creates a trust and transfers property to it is generally called the *grantor*. A grantor is sometimes called a *settlor, maker, donor,* or *trustor*. The person who presently benefits from the trust is the *beneficiary* and the person who will benefit from the trust after the beneficiary dies is the *remainder beneficiary*.

Beneficiaries and remainder beneficiaries can be corporations or non-profit institutions or charities. Beneficiaries may be given different rights in the trust property. Some beneficiaries may be *income beneficiaries* and be entitled to receive only the income from the trust property. This may be interest from a savings account or bond, dividends from stock, rental income from real estate, etc. Other beneficiaries may be *principal beneficiaries* and be entitled to receive the actual trust assets—for example, the money in the savings account, the bond, stock or rental real estate. Sometimes the beneficiary may receive both income and principal.

The person in charge of managing the trust, who often times is the same person who created the trust, is called a *trustee*. In most states, any person or entity (bank, trust company, and some brokerage firms) who is capable of taking legal title to property can be appointed trustee. Trustees have a legal duty (often called a fiduciary duty) to protect the assets of the trust and make certain that the purposes of the trust as stated in the trust document are carried out. The grantor spells out the powers of the trustee in the trust document. Each state also has specific laws that govern the conduct of trustees to ensure that the trust assets are protected, the purposes of the trust are honored, and the beneficiaries of the trust are protected.

Each trust should also designate a *successor* or *alternate* trustee. This person or entity will take over the management of the trust if the original trustee dies or becomes unable to continue management of the trust. If a successor trustee is not named, the court has authority to name a successor trustee if one is needed.

Examples.

1. Bob and Helen transfer property to a trust and name Ross as trustee. The trust document states that the income from the trust,

will be paid to Bob and Helen until their death and then it shall be paid to Chrissy.

2. Joe transfers property to a trust and names Jane as trustee. Joe's trust document states that the income from the trust will be paid to Robert until he reaches age thirty and when Robert reaches age thirty the trust principal will be distributed to Gail.

3. Dan transfers property to a trust and names Dorothy as trustee. The trust provides that Dan's three grandchildren will be beneficiaries of the income and principal of the trust until they complete college. At that time the trust will end and the trust property will be divided equally among Dan's children.

Often grantors name alternate beneficiaries to receive the trust property if the original beneficiary cannot receive the trust property.

Testamentary trusts are created under the terms of a person's will and take effect only when the person dies. Such trusts by their very nature do not avoid probate. The trusts are subject to the supervision of the court and the trustee must periodically file reports with the court to account for the income earned by the trust, the taxes and expenses paid by the trust, and the distributions of income and principal made to the beneficiaries. These reports can be costly to prepare.

Inter vivos trusts (most commonly known as living trusts) take effect during a person's lifetime. Such trusts are created under the terms of a special document separate from the person's will. Property is transferred to the trust and managed by the trustee. Most grantors of living trusts name themselves as trustee during their lifetime. This permits them to continue to manage their assets just as they had before the assets were transferred into the living trust. The grantor/trustee typically names himself as income and principal beneficiary during lifetime and designates the individuals who will receive the income and principal after he or she dies.

IRREVOCABLE
TRUSTS

Living trusts can be revocable or irrevocable. A revocable living trust can be changed or terminated by the grantor during his or her life. At the death of the grantor, the trust becomes irrevocable. An irrevocable trust cannot be changed or terminated. A grantor who wants to retain complete control over the property that he or she transferred to the trust and change the trust during his or her lifetime should make certain to include a provision in the trust document that states the trust is revocable.

Why would someone set up a trust that they could not change or revoke? Because such a trust can avoid taxes and in some cases can be safe from creditors' claims.

Examples.

1. Nancy is involved in an automobile accident and the insurance company for the person who caused the accident offers her a million dollars. She accepts the award on the condition that it be set up in an irrevocable trust for herself and her daughter. Years later Nancy commits malpractice. The victim of her malpractice cannot touch her trust because it is irrevocable.

2. Ben owns a valuable piece of property he bought many years ago. He knows that on his death it will add a million dollars to his estate and that 55% of the value will have to be paid in estate taxes. Ben sets up a charitable remainder trust and donates the property to the trust. With careful planning and the use of life insurance, the property will go to the American Heart Association upon Ben's death and his children will receive a million dollars tax-free.

While irrevocable trusts can offer some excellent benefits, they must be set up carefully to be effective. If you feel your estate would benefit from such a trust you should consult an expert in the field.

The Living Trust 3

In the previous chapter you were introduced to the basic elements of a trust and to the distinction between living trusts and testamentary trusts. Living trusts have become very popular as a probate avoidance alternative. In fact, living trusts are perhaps the most efficient and effective method to avoid probate and pass assets quickly to beneficiaries without incurring substantial probate and attorney fees.

Living trusts are legal "will substitutes" recognized in all states. The living trust is a legal entity that can own, hold and distribute assets to trust beneficiaries. A living trust is created by a legal document and is funded when legal title to assets is transferred to the trustee. It is a revocable trust that can be changed or amended by the grantor during his or her life. The living trust is called that because it comes into existence while the grantor is living and, when assets are transferred to the trust to be distributed as the trust document directs, the trust "comes to life." After the grantor's death the trust becomes irrevocable—it cannot be changed or cancelled.

Advantages of a Living Trust

Living trusts offer several advantages that wills do not.

AVOIDANCE OF PROBATE

Assets placed in a living trust prior to your death don't go through the probate process. This can save your estate several thousand dollars in probate costs (including the cost of an executor's bond), attorney fees, and appraiser fees. Because the assets in a living trust are not subject to the delays of the probate process, they can be distributed quickly and efficiently to the beneficiaries. Generally, the trustee will only require proof of your death and then will begin to manage the trust assets and distribute them according to the terms of the trust document.

FLEXIBILITY

Because the living trust is revocable it can be changed or cancelled at anytime and for any reason. If your family circumstances change, for instance if you divorce or if you or a family member becomes ill, or if a beneficiary dies, a living trust can be easily amended. Also, if you move from state to state, the trust will be valid in all states. Wills, by contrast, can be changed or cancelled but generally the process is more time consuming and expensive because the strict state laws governing the creation and amendment of wills impose many burdens on the person making the will.

PRIVACY

A living trust is totally confidential. It is not subject to disclosure to the probate court as is a will. Wills become public documents and can be read by anyone who takes the time and has the interest to do so. Also, when a will is probated the court will require that a listing or inventory of the probate assets be filed. These inventories may also be public documents that reveal the assets that comprise the estate. This is not the case with a living trust. Neither the assets in the trust at the time of death nor the terms of the trust and the identities of the beneficiaries are required to be disclosed to the public. The only persons who need to be aware of the trust's existence, its assets and its terms are you, the trustee and the beneficiaries.

There are some states that require a trust to be registered with the court where the trustee lives or administers the trust. The trustee must file certain information with the court including the name of the grantor, the name of the trustee, the date on which the trust was created, and some form of written acceptance of the trusts by the trustee. This acceptance is often evidenced by the trustee's signature on the trust document.

Failure of the trustee to register the trusts generally doesn't result in legal consequences or penalties. This registration requirement impacts and undercuts the privacy advantage of the living trust. As of the date this book was written, the following states have laws governing the registration of living trusts:

Alaska	Maine
Colorado	Michigan
Florida	Missouri
Hawaii	Nebraska
Idaho	North Dakota

CONTROL

While you are alive, you continue to manage and control the assets in the trust just as you did prior to establishing the trust. You continue to direct how the assets will be invested and how the assets will be used during your lifetime. Of course, if you choose to designate someone other than yourself to handle the investment of the assets you may either name that person as trustee or hire that person to give you investment advice. In a living trust you will personally select the successor trustee who will control your assets. The living trust will contain your specific instructions regarding how the assets are to be invested and distributed. Property passing through the probate process is subject to the many complex state laws imposing rules on executors which often limit the investments and distributions executors can make.

ORDERLINESS

A living trust will help you to keep your financial affairs in order and the records in a central location. This saves your family a great deal of time after your death attempting to locate and identify your assets.

CONTESTABILITY	Trusts are generally more difficult for unhappy heirs to contest than wills.
DISABILITY	Perhaps the second most important advantage of a living trust is the avoidance of a court supervised guardianship in the event you become incapacitated due to stroke, senility, or other form of mental incompetency. One in four Americans will experience some form of disability that lasts more than three months. The average disability lasts over a year. Ordinarily, when a disability occurs a guardian must be appointed by the court and the guardian must manage your assets through strict court supervised procedures. Many times the guardian appointed by the court is not the person you would have chosen to manage your assets. If your assets are placed in your living trust before your incapacity, the expense and delay of a guardianship is avoided. The trustee of your trust would step into your shoes and manage your assets.
OUT-OF-STATE PROPERTIES	If you live in Illinois and own real estate in Florida, upon your death your executor must begin two probate proceedings—one in Illinois to deal with your assets located in Illinois and one in Florida to deal with the transfer of title to the real estate located in Florida. However, if the out of state property is placed in your living trust, upon your death such property will not be subject to probate either in Illinois or Florida.
CONTINUATION OF BUSINESS	Living trusts are very useful to business owners. Whether the business is a sole proprietorship or a corporation, the business owner can transfer the business assets to the living trust. If the owner becomes disabled or dies, the successor trustee can step into the owner's shoes and handle the day to day affairs of the business without an interruption in the business. Because many times a business is a primary source of income to the owner and his or her family, after the owner's death or disability it is critical that the business continue to operate and generate the income needed to support the owner's family.

Disadvantages of a Living Trust

While living trusts offer many advantages there are some drawbacks to a living trust. While some of those listed below, such as no tax savings, may not be disadvantages over a will, they are disadvantages over doing more extensive estate planning.

No Income Tax Savings

The living trust does not avoid or save income taxes while you are alive. Because you have retained control of the assets in the living trust, you receive the benefits of the trust and you are both the grantor and trustee of the trust, the income earned by the trust assets will be taxed to you. You will be required to report any income earned by the trust on your personal income tax return, Form 1040. No separate return has to be filed for the trust. After your death, the trust will be required to obtain its own taxpayer identification number from the Internal Revenue Service. This is done by filing Form SS-4 with the District Director of Internal Revenue. A copy of Form SS-4 is included in appendix B. The trust will be required to file its own tax return, Form 1041, each year if the trust had "any taxable income," or had "gross income" of $600.00 or more, regardless of the amount of "taxable income" in any one year. Thus, even a trust that owns only tax exempt bonds that pay over $600.00 worth of interest during a year will have to file a tax return. A copy of Form 1041 is included in appendix B. On the following page is a chart illustrating how income earned by the trust is reported on your individual tax return, (Form 1040).

INCOME TAX REPORTING OUTLINE:

```
┌──────────┐   ┌──────────┐   ┌──────────┐
│ Dividends│   │ Interest │   │  Rents   │
└────┬─────┘   └────┬─────┘   └────┬─────┘
     └──────────────┼──────────────┘
              ┌──────┴──────┐
              │ JOHN DOE TRUST │
              │(full name required)│
              └──────┬──────┘
              ┌──────┴──────┐
              │  John Doe   │
              └──────┬──────┘
                Form 1040
```

NO ESTATE TAX SAVINGS

At your death, federal estate taxes will be due if the value of your probate and non-probate assets exceeds the amount of the unified credit. Many states also impose their own estate or death taxes. If you are married and the value of the estates of you and your spouse is over the amount of the unified credit there are special planning techniques that can be used to help eliminate in whole or in part the estate taxes that would be due from you and your spouse's estates. If you and your spouse's estates are worth more than the amount of the unified credit and you want to avoid estate taxes, then you should consult with an experienced estate tax professional. If the value of your estate exceeds the amount of the unified credit, then your executor will be required to file a federal estate tax return with the Internal Revenue Service. The first four pages of the federal estate tax return, Form 706, are included in appendix B.

MORE COMPLEX AND EXPENSIVE THAN A WILL

If you hire an attorney to set up a living trust for you the expense will be greater than for a will. If you create your own living trust the most complex aspect of the process will be transferring your assets to the trust. Once your assets are transferred to the trust you will have to keep separate trust records and not mix them with any personal accounts you have such as joint accounts or pay on death accounts.

NO DEADLINES FOR CLAIMS OF CREDITORS

When a will is probated (or an estate without a will is probated), a deadline is imposed on creditors of the decedent. Creditors are required to present their claim to the executor of the estate within a time period specified by statute. Each state has its own statute establishing this time period. It can range from three months to one year. These statutes also establish the procedures that a creditor must follow to present its claim. If a creditor does not follow the procedures within the statutory time period, the creditor loses its right to the assets of the estate and is forever prohibited from suing the estate to collect the assets due it. In most states, however, a living trust is not subject to such statutory procedures. Therefore, a creditor can sue the trust or its beneficiaries for amounts due it long after you have died. Even after the trust has terminated and all of the trust assets are distributed to the beneficiaries, creditors can sue the beneficiaries for claims it has against you.

DOES NOT AVOID CREDITOR CLAIMS DURING YOUR LIFE

A revocable living trust does not prevent your creditors from suing you or suing your trust to collect debts during your lifetime. Because you have maintained complete control over the trust assets, the courts treat you as the owner of the assets and can force you to pay trust assets to your creditors. If you know that you owe a creditor money and you transfer all of your assets to your trust in an attempt to keep them away from your creditor, the courts will view the transfer as a fraudulent conveyance and may force you not only to pay the creditor but also pay a fine.

DOES NOT ELIMINATE THE NEED FOR A WILL

As was discussed in chapter 1, even though you have a living trust that is funded with all of your assets during your lifetime, it is important to also have a will. The will can name a guardian for your children, appoint an executor of your probate estate and provide that no bond be required of your executor. There may be assets that you have forgotten to transfer to your trust, an unexpected inheritance, or a lawsuit that must be filed on behalf of your estate after your death and a will covers these assets even if the will only provides that such assets "pour-over" to your living trust. Without the will, you will have died "intestate" and must follow the probate procedures for intestacy. Intestacy procedures are complex, time consuming and generally very expensive.

LIVING TRUST VS. OTHER PROBATE ALTERNATIVES

In chapter 2 other probate alternatives were described. Each of these probate alternatives accomplishes most people's primary goal: avoid the costs and delay of probate at death. The living trust accomplishes this goal and has the additional advantages discussed above. But the living trust has a very important advantage over the other probate alternatives. The living trust collects all of your assets in one place. This greatly simplifies the management and investment of your assets and makes it much easier for you to keep track of who you have named as the beneficiaries of your estate. If a beneficiary dies, or if you decide no longer to include them in your estate, you simply have to amend the trust to remove the beneficiary. You do not have to change every account of which person is a beneficiary or a joint tenant. Also, if you become incapacitated, the successor trustee can take over the management of your assets and avoid a guardianship. In the case of joint tenancy property, you would have to trust the joint tenant to use the funds for your benefit.

Even though a living trust has some disadvantages, they are greatly outweighed by the many advantages of a living trust. The cost savings of avoiding probate during your life if you become incapacitated and after your death and the peace of mind that you gain by knowing that the assets you worked your lifetime to accumulate will pass to your beneficiaries quickly and as you intended after your death should leave no question in your mind that a living trust is for you.

CREATING YOUR LIVING TRUST 4

A living trust is created by a written document that is clear and specific. It does not have to contain fancy legal terms. The living trust document will serve as the road map describing how you want your assets to be distributed during your lifetime and after your death. You need to identify the trustees, the beneficiaries and the trust assets.

In chapter 2 the parties to a trust (grantor, trustee, and beneficiary) were described. When you write your trust it is important to identify each of these parties so that it is absolutely clear who they are. The beneficiary should not be identified as your "spouse" or "Mrs. John Smith." Instead, you should use "my spouse, Mary Smith" to identify your spouse. Often it is helpful to include not only the person's legal name but something else to clearly identify the person such as an address or social security number.

In order to create a valid trust, the trust document must be signed by you and the trustee. Although not required in all states, the trust should be notarized by a notary public, particularly if you plan to transfer real estate to the trust. You must also transfer property to the trust when you sign the trust document. This property can be money, securities, real estate, automobiles, personal property and the like. Chapter 5 describes how your assets can be transferred to your trust. A trust can be created with as little as $10 in it. If you are not ready to transfer all of your assets to the trust, you can simply attach a $10 bill to your signed trust document and your trust will come "alive."

Before you create your living trust, you should take a few moments to complete the ESTATE PLANNING WORKSHEET (Form 3). This worksheet will help you collect all of the information you need to create and fund your living trust. The worksheet will also be helpful to your family because it will identify your assets which saves your family the time consuming process of collecting such information after your death. If you find that your total assets, including life insurance benefits and retirement plans, exceed the amount of the unified credit, and you wish to minimize your estate taxes, you should seek the advice of an experienced professional.

Four basic living trust forms are included in this book. Forms 4 and 5 are living trusts that can be used by a married individual. Forms 6 and 7 can be used by a single individual. The provisions contained in these Forms are the most popular among persons interested in establishing living trusts. Of course, the distribution provisions can be changed to reflect your individual intentions.

THE TRUSTEE

When you create your living trust you will be the initial trustee. It is important to name at least one and preferably two alternate trustees. One or both of these trustees will step into your shoes in the event you cannot serve as trustee. Generally, for married couples, the spouse is named as the first alternate trustee. This permits you to maintain total control over your assets. Parents, brothers, sisters or other trusted family members may also be named as alternate trustees. You may also have a friend that you trust and wish to name as trustee. Some people like to name an institution such as a bank or trust company to serve as alternate trustee if all of the persons you name as alternates are unable to serve as trustee. However, you should check the institution's fee schedule. Some charge fees which are outrageously high and some will not accept a trust if it does not have a minimum value.

A trust is a contract or agreement between the grantor and the trustee. It is important that you talk to the alternate trustees and get their permission in advance to name them as trustees. If you did not get their permission and all of the alternates decline to serve, the court would have to appoint an alternate trustee. The person or institution appointed may not be one you would have chosen. If an institution is appointed to serve, the fee it charges will reduce the amount of your assets that pass to your beneficiaries. It takes little time to make certain that you have named alternate trustees who are willing to serve.

If you decide to name two or more individuals to serve as trustee together, to be *co-trustees*, generally all of them must agree before any investments or distributions can be made. Some states require that only the agreement of a majority of the trustees is necessary. Some grantors give one trustee a veto power or a tie-breaking power.

Sometimes a person you may want to serve as trustee may have a lot of knowledge about investments and property management but may not be responsive to the needs of others, namely the trust beneficiaries. In contrast, you may have in mind a person who is very understanding about the needs of beneficiaries having had children of their own but who has no investment management skills. You can name both of these people as trustees and designate the primary role that each will play as trustee. The investment-wise individual may have the final word with regard to transactions involving the investment of trust property and the other individual may be given the final word with regard to the nature and timing of distributions to the beneficiaries.

As you decide who to name as alternate trustees, it is important to understand a trustee's duties and powers.

DUTIES OF A TRUSTEE

Each state has laws that impose certain duties on trustees. If the trustee does not fulfill his or her duties, he or she is said to have *breached his or her duty* and he or she can be sued by the grantor or a beneficiary. If the trustee loses the lawsuit he or she can be made to pay money to the beneficiaries or grantor to recover losses the trust suffered while he or she served. He or she can also be removed from his or her position as trustee.

Possession and control of trust assets. A trustee must collect and take possession of trust property as quickly as possible after he or she becomes a trustee. This does not mean that the trustee must take actual physical possession of the trust property. He or she must, however, take whatever steps are necessary to take control of the assets. For instance, the trustee does not have to take actual possession of the stock certificates held by a brokerage firm. Instead, the trustee must make certain that the legal title to the stock is transferred into the name of the trust and that the trustee is authorized to deal with the stocks.

Preservation of trust assets. After the trustee has located and taken control of the trust assets, the trustee must preserve and protect the trust assets. The trustee must make certain that the trust assets are not wasting away or in danger of losing value. For instance, if the trust includes interests in a family business, the trustee must make certain that the business is being managed appropriately and that there is no interruption in the business. You certainly would not want to lose business customers and lose not only the income of the business but also the reputation that the business has developed.

Investment of trust assets. The trustee must invest and maintain the trust assets so that they produce income for the benefit of the beneficiaries. A trust is not established with the idea that trust assets will be idle and not produce income that can be given to the beneficiaries. Traditionally, almost every state required that a trustee adhere to the *prudent man rule* with regard to investing trust assets. The prudent man rule requires the trustee to invest, reinvest, supervise and manage trust property using the judgment and care that persons of ordinary prudence, discretion and intelligence would use with regard to their own property. Trustees are generally authorized to acquire and keep every kind of property, real, personal and mixed, and every kind of investment, including bonds, stocks, securities, real estate partnerships and the like.

Under the prudent man rule a trustee should:

- ☞ Diversify the trust assets among many types of investments such as stocks, bonds, etc.;

- ☞ Diversify among various industries with his or her stock holdings;

- ☞ Consider current income as well as long-term increase in value of the asset since the beneficiaries of income and those who will eventually receive trust principal may not be the same; and

- ☞ Seek professional advice for initial investment and continuing review of investments.

Under the prudent man rule a trustee should not:

- ☞ Invest in risky ventures hoping to make a "big killing";

- ☞ Lend trust property to himself individually except at fair value and with the consent of the beneficiary (or all beneficiaries);

- ☞ Buy assets from the trust except at appraised value;

- ☞ Continue to hold investments which a prudent man would no longer hold;

- ☞ Continue to hold investments transferred to the trust without independently investigating their quality; and

- ☞ Delegate investment decisions to others. It is acceptable to seek advice from others but ultimately the trustee must make the actual investment decisions.

While most states still use the prudent man rule, some states (such as Florida) are adopting what is being called the *prudent expert rule*. This requires the trustee to use "the care, skill, prudence and diligence under the circumstances then prevailing that a prudent person acting in a like capacity and familiar with such matters would use in the conduct of an enterprise of a like character and with like aims." This may result in a greater likelihood of a trustee being liable for a bad investment, and in someone being a bit reluctant to serve as a trustee. With most of the forms in this book, you or your spouse will be serving as trustee or alternatively, will be closely supervising the trustee so there should be few, if any, problems with regard to the trust investments. In all of the forms included in this book, the trustee is given broad discretion with regard to investment authority. The trustee by state law will be bound by the prudent man rule or the prudent expert rule. If you wish to restrict the investment power of the trustee you may want to add a provision or do a trust amendment that contains specific investment guidelines for the trustee. These guidelines could limit investments to stock in Fortune 500 companies, bonds with a minimum credit rating, prohibit investment in real estate ventures, etc. However, you must be careful and try to think far off into the future when you limit the trustee's investment power. The trustee needs some degree of flexibility to take into account the changing economic and investment situations. For example, David established a trust in the early 1980s when certificates of deposit were earning about fifteen percent or more. David limited the trustee's investment power to "certificates of deposit and any other financial instrument backed by the U.S. government with comparable interest rates." Because interest rates on CDs are now yielding only five percent, they would no longer be a good investment.

Inform beneficiaries. The trustee must also inform the trust beneficiaries of the existence of the trust and explain its provisions. To do this the trustee himself must understand all of the trust's provisions. Because the trust is a private document between the grantor and the trustee (which usually is the grantor himself), the beneficiaries will often not be aware of the trust's existence until after the grantor dies or becomes incapacitated.

Accounting. The trustee has a responsibility to report to the beneficiaries and keep them informed of all of the trust transactions. This includes reporting all assets received, sold or exchanged by the trust,

income earned and expenses incurred and distributions made to beneficiaries. The date, amount and a short explanation of each transaction
should be included in the reports. These reports can be done on a
monthly, quarterly or annual basis. You may include a specific
instruction in the trust as to how frequently these reports must be given
or you may leave it to the trustee to determine the frequency of such
reports.

Keep trust assets separate. Importantly, the trustee must keep the trust
assets separate from his or her own assets. The trust assets must be
clearly identified and titles to bank accounts, stocks, etc. should have the
name of the trustee, as trustee, on them. Income earned by the trust
assets must be kept separate as well. Failure to do this is called *com-
mingling* and is one of the primary reasons lawsuits are brought against
trustees.

Trustees should never borrow assets from the trust, sell assets to the
trust, or purchase or lease assets from the trust for his or her own purposes unless it is at fair value with written consent of all beneficiaries.

Make distributions. Finally, the trustee must make distributions to the
trust beneficiaries as provided in the trust document. The trustee is not
allowed to substitute his or her judgment for the terms of the trust. If
the trust permits the trustee to use his or her discretion in making distributions to the beneficiaries, the trustee must be reasonable in his or
her decisions. For instance, it would be inappropriate for a trustee to
favor one beneficiary over the other when making distributions simply
because the trustee doesn't like the beneficiary or doesn't agree with
how the beneficiary behaves.

TRUSTEE
POWERS

Each state has specific laws giving trustees powers to administer the
trust. As creator of the trust, you can broaden the scope of these powers
or you may restrict the powers. For example, you may wish to prohibit
the trustee from selling the vacation home you inherited from your parents. The powers often given to trustees under state law include the
power to invest and sell assets, the power to collect income and rents,

the power to invest in stocks and real estate, open bank accounts, join in litigation to protect the trust assets, and hire professionals such as accountants and attorneys to assist the trustee in fulfilling his or her duties.

You can grant a trustee special powers such as the power to distribute funds to beneficiaries before the normal time for a distribution if the trustee believes that the beneficiary is in need of the funds.

If you wish to limit the type of investments that a trustee can make you must be very specific in the trust document. If you do not leave clear instructions, the trustee can unknowingly undermine your intentions.

REMOVING A
TRUSTEE

Sometimes it is important to be able to remove a trustee without having to involve the court. Generally, the trust document gives the grantor the right to remove the trustee and name an alternate trustee. You may wish to include a provision in the trust giving your beneficiaries or a third party the power to remove a trustee if the trustee is stealing from the trust, is not fulfilling his or her duties under the law, or is not following the terms of the trust document.

A trustee may also voluntarily choose to quit. If your trust does not contain instructions on how a trustee can resign, the trustee must obtain the approval of the court to resign. The beneficiaries cannot simply agree to accept the trustee's resignation.

If your trust does not name an alternate trustee, you or the trust beneficiaries must petition the court to appoint an alternate trustee.

BENEFICIARIES

When you establish your living trust you must decide who will be the beneficiaries of the trust, how much each beneficiary will receive and when the beneficiaries will receive their gift from the trust.

While you are alive, you will be the primary beneficiary of your living trust. You may also wish to name your spouse and minor children as beneficiaries while you are alive. Then, if you become incapacitated, the successor trustee can make distributions not only for your care but also for the care of your spouse and minor children. This is particularly important if you are the primary income earner. Your trust assets will earn income that can assist your family as it adjusts to the loss of your paycheck.

You may name beneficiaries to receive income only, principal only (principal is the property you transfer to the trust), or both income and principal. After your death, you may wish to give all of trust property to your spouse with the intention that she assume your role and provide for herself and your children. If your spouse has established a living trust of her own, the trust assets can be distributed directly to her living trust.

If you do not have a spouse, or if you believe that your spouse has sufficient assets to take care of herself, and you want to name your children as beneficiaries you have several options available to you.

Lump sum distribution. You may wish to distribute all of the trust assets to your children at one time, in a single lump sum, after your death.

Delayed distribution of single trust. Most parents want to be certain that there are enough funds available to provide for their children until they reach a certain age. (For example, when the youngest child has completed college.) You can accomplish this by keeping all of the trust property in a single fund and giving the trustee discretion to make distributions to each child as he or she needs funds just as you would do. Thus, as medical or tuition bills need to be paid, the trustee can make distributions either directly to the child or to the doctor or college to pay these bills. Generally, such discretionary distributions are limited to food, clothing, shelter, health care, education and special events such as weddings. When the youngest child reaches the age you specify, the remaining trust property can be divided equally among the children and distributed to them. The trust will then terminate.

Delayed distribution of separate trusts. Alternatively, the trust can immediately separate into equal shares after your death, one for each child. The trustee can make distributions to the child for the same reasons described above. Such distributions would be entirely within the discretion of the trustee. The trustee can also make periodic distributions to the child at scheduled intervals—monthly, quarterly or annually. This provides the beneficiary with a regular income. Of course, you can combine the two methods and provide a regular income and, to the extent the regular income does not fulfill the needs of the child, the trustee can make additional distributions to the child.

As long as the trustee alone has the decision making power with regard to when distributions (other than the periodic distributions) will be made and for what purpose, the creditors of the child cannot touch the trust property.

Staggered distributions. You may also provide that distributions of principal be staggered to your children. For example, your living trust may provide that distributions be made to your child quarterly and that the trustee may make additional distributions to the child if he or she is in need. Instead of distributing all of the trust property at once, you can provide, for example, that one-third of the trust property be distributed to the child at age twenty-five, one-third at age thirty and the remaining trust property at age thirty-five. This allows the trust to terminate over time while not sacrificing the needs of the child. You can decide on the ages and percentages as you create your living trust.

Whichever method of distribution you use you should be careful to avoid making distributions contingent on the happening of a certain event. For instance, you should not provide that distributions will be made when a child gets married, graduates from a particular college, has a child, etc. These restrictions may keep a child from ever receiving the trust property. Remember, children are different from each other and even from their parents. Don't put restrictions in your trust that force your child to live up to expectations that cannot be changed after you have died.

Rule against perpetuities. If you decide to keep the property in trust for the benefit of your children or other beneficiaries, you should be aware of a rule governing the length of time that property can be held in trust. This rule is called the *rule against perpetuities*. The rule prohibits a trust grantor from controlling the distribution of trust property for too long. To prevent trusts from extending several generations and keeping family wealth tied up for extremely long periods of time, the rule against perpetuities states that a trust cannot keep property for longer than the life of any person living when the trust was created plus twenty-one years. At that time, the full ownership rights in the trust property must be given to the beneficiaries. Most people do not have to concern themselves with this rule but most trust documents contain a clause to make sure that the rule against perpetuities is not violated.

Death of a beneficiary before distribution. What happens if a beneficiary dies before you do or dies before his or her share of the trust is completely distributed to him or her? Most parents would like their grandchildren to be provided for and inherit the property their parent would have received. Lawyers commonly use either the phrase *per capita* or *per stirpes* in the clause specifying how the property will be distributed.

Per capita distributions are pro rata or *share and share alike* distributions. That means that all of the surviving descendants, regardless of generation, get equal shares of the trust property.

Example.

> Michael has four grown children, George, Tom, Judy and Karen. Karen has three children and she dies before Michael. At Michael's death the trust property is to be distributed per capita. The trust property will be distributed in six equal shares—one for each living child of Michael and one for each of Karen's children.

Per stirpes distributions are by representation. This means that if one of your children dies before you do, the amount that beneficiary would have received is divided equally among that beneficiary's direct descendants.

Example.

> Same facts as above, but at Michael's death the trust property would be divided into four equal shares—one for each of his children and one to be subdivided among Karen's three children.

All of the above examples and discussion applies not only to your children but to any beneficiaries that you name. Remember, the living trust identifies who you want to receive your property, how much, and when. You can design the living trust any way you want to make sure that your intentions are carried out.

Specific gifts. You may chose to leave certain assets to selected beneficiaries. For instance, you may want your oldest child to receive the vacation home that has been in your family. Or you may want your daughter to receive your jewelry. You can include these specific gifts in your living trust.

Sometimes the list of specific gifts may be lengthy. Rather than include all of the specific gifts in your trust you may leave a written memorandum in addition to your living trust that lists the specific items of your tangible personal property to be distributed. Your living trust must, however, refer to this memorandum. The forms included in this book refers to the memorandum. If you choose not to leave specific gifts you do not need to complete the memorandum. If you wish to change the specific gifts, you can simply change the memorandum and do not have to sign an entire new trust document. A memorandum with instructions is included in appendix A as Form 8. This memorandum should not be used for real estate, stocks, bonds, or anything other than tangible personal items. Such specific gifts should be included in your living trust document.

Charitable beneficiaries. If you would like to leave a gift to your church or some other charitable organization, you can include a provision in your trust giving such organization a specified dollar amount or a percentage of the assets in the trust. Remember, your living trust acts as a will substitute, so any gifts you would have included in your will you can include in your trust.

There may be special circumstances that require your living trust to contain unique provisions. For instance, you may wish to provide for a disabled or special needs child or you may have a child who is financially irresponsible and needs more restrictions on his or her share. You may have children from two marriages and wish to provide for them differently. Your parents may depend upon you for support and would require continued financial assistance after your death. With the help of an experienced professional, your living trust can be designed to address such special circumstances. The forms contained in this book provide the most common and basic trust alternatives. You should not expect to use these forms for such circumstances.

Gifts to pets. Except in California and Tennessee you cannot leave property to your pets. This is because a pet is property, and property cannot own other property. If you wish to have a pet cared for after your death you should make arrangements with a person you trust and leave them money for that purpose. Otherwise you might be able to sign up for a life care contract with an animal shelter or veterinarian.

SIGNING YOUR LIVING TRUST

Now that you have designed your living trust by choosing your alternate trustees, your beneficiaries, and the distribution pattern of trust property, you must sign the trust document and fund the trust. You should sign the trust document as both the grantor and trustee. Three witnesses should watch you sign the trust document and sign the document themselves (most states only require two witnesses, but a few require three). All of this should be done in the presence of a notary public who should sign and notarize the living trust (notary requirements may also vary from state to state, but your notary should know how to modify the forms to meet these requirements). To get started, you should fund the trust with $10 by attaching a $10 bill to the last page of the trust document. Now you are ready to transfer assets to your trust. Later the $10 can be deposited into the trust bank account.

AMENDING YOUR LIVING TRUST

After you have signed your living trust, events may occur that make you want to change your living trust. For example, a successor trustee may die or change his or her mind about serving as trustee, you may wish to add or remove a beneficiary, or you may wish to change the requirements for distributions of trust assets. Your living trust can be easily amended to reflect these changes. You do not have to draft an entire new living trust. Instead, you can do an amendment to the trust that only makes the change that you desire. Form 9 can be used for amending your trust.

 If you wish to cancel your living trust in the future, you can use Form 10 for this purpose. When the trust is canceled, you will have to "unfund" your trust and transfer all of the assets out of the trust and back to yourself in your individual name or into joint accounts or other arrangements as discussed in chapter 2.

FAMILY LIMITED PARTNERSHIPS

One of the increasing popular ways to avoid probate is the family limited partnership. There are many tax and non-tax advantages associated with family limited partnerships. The most common objectives of family limited partnerships are: protection of assets from future creditors;

consolidation of asset ownership and management; family wealth accumulation; and flexibility.

A limited partnership is similar to a corporation in that its assets are owned by various individuals who have an ownership interest in the limited partnership. Each individual owner is called a *partner*. There are two different categories of partners: limited partners and general partners. The basic, and very important difference between these two categories of partners is that in the event of a lawsuit against the partnership, the limited partner's exposure to loss is limited to his or her investment in the partnership—the money or property that the limited partner contributed to the partnership. A general partner, however, may lose not only his or her investment in the partnership, but all of his or her other assets as well.

Some of the features of a limited partnership include:

Asset protection. In the event of a lawsuit against a partner individually, all of the partner's investment assets, including real estate, would be exposed to seizure by the suing party. If these assets are owned by a family limited partnership, creditors could not reach the assets themselves. Instead, creditors could only attach the limited partnership interest. A properly constructed family partnership would prevent a limited partner from causing the termination of the partnership thereby protecting the underlying assets from a creditor-forced distribution. The creditor of a limited partner may obtain a charging order which gives the creditor the right to the income portion of the limited partner's interest. However, the general partner may decide not to authorize distribution of income to the limited partners. Therefore, a creditor may have a responsibility for federal income tax liability attributable to the limited partnership interest, yet have limited or no rights to receive actual distributions from the partnership. Since the creditor may be responsible for the liability of paying taxes on "phantom" income, and yet not acquire partnership assets or take part in partnership management (which is usually vested in the general partner), creditors generally are not interested in obtaining limited partnership interests. This protects the partnership's assets and preserves them for distribution to family members in the future.

Consolidation of asset ownership and management. All of the investment assets are brought under the ownership of one entity—the limited partnership. Family members are not given fractional interests in stock, real estate, and the like. Consolidation of the investments reduces the need for more than one money manager and more than one investment account and likely results in a reduction of fees. The general partner is typically vested with the authority to manage the partnership's affairs which includes employing investment advisors and money managers.

Family wealth accumulation. Family partnership agreements are often drafted with buy-sell provisions to help make certain that the assets will remain in the family. If a family member attempts to assign his or her interest in the partnership to a non-family member, the partnership agreement may provide that the other partners or the partnership has the right to acquire the assigned partnership interest on the same terms as the proposed assignment. This permits the wealth generated by the investments to accrue to the benefit of the family. This often becomes important when there exists a fear of protecting one's children from the consequences of divorce in a community property state such as Texas.

Flexibility. The limited partnership agreement is a flexible document. If all of the partners agree, the partnership agreement may be amended or terminated. In contrast, an irrevocable trust generally cannot be amended or terminated without participation by a court and a guardian ad litem or a lawyer. A partnership may generally be terminated without adverse tax consequences but there may be severe tax consequences upon the termination of a corporation. Additionally, a limited partnership provides greater investment flexibility because of the operation of the business judgment rule. The prudent person rule, which applies to trustees, is a stricter standard than the business judgment rule which applies to managing partners of a partnership.

Example.

Joe and Kathy transfer their property to a family limited partnership. The partnership agreement provides that the income will be paid to Joe and Kathy during their lifetimes in such amounts determined by the general partner. Joe and Kathy set up a trust, which they control, to be the general partner. Joe and Kathy pay all of the income to themselves each year. When Joe is involved in an automobile accident and is sued, no income is paid to Joe until the lawsuit is settled.

Family limited partnerships provide many benefits. However, they must be set up carefully to make certain that the benefits are enjoyed by the partners. Consultation with an expert in this field of planning is a must.

FUNDING YOUR LIVING TRUST 5

The primary purpose for creating your living trust is to avoid probate during your lifetime (such as during an incapacity) and after your death. In order to accomplish this, you must transfer legal title to your property to the trust and thereby transform it into non-probate property.

HOW MUCH PROPERTY SHOULD I TRANSFER?

There is no rule telling you how much or which property you should transfer to the trust. Obviously, the more property transferred to the trust, the less is subject to the expense and delay of probate after your death. Often, it is advisable to keep some cash in a JTWROS checking account with a bank. Grocery stores, department stores and the like are not familiar with checks drawn on trust accounts and signed by trustees. Rather than deal with the hassles caused by a store clerk who hesitates or refuses to accept a trust check, it is advisable to keep at least one bank account outside of the trust. However, if possible and practical, you should use some form of joint tenancy or POD account to avoid subjecting the property to probate at your death.

How Is Title Held for Trust Assets?

Most property transferred to your living trust must be retitled in the name of the trust. The basic title that is recommended for use in holding all assets in the trust is:

```
[YOUR NAME], trustee, [YOUR NAME] Trust, dated _____, _____.
```

For example:

```
JOHN DOE, trustee, JOHN DOE TRUST, dated January 23, 1999.
```

Some institutions may require slightly different wording. However, the name of the trust, the name of the trustee, and the date the trust was created are normally all that is required.

How Do I Transfer Property to My Living Trust?

PERSONAL PROPERTY
You can transfer personal belongings such as furniture, antiques, artwork, clothing, jewelry and the like to the trust by signing an ASSIGNMENT OF PERSONAL PROPERTY (Form 10). This form should be notarized.

AUTOMOBILES
Automobiles have title certificates that must be changed. You can contact your local government agency that handles motor vehicle registrations to obtain the correct forms to accomplish this. Also, contact your automobile insurance company to make sure that the owner on your policy is changed. Such a transfer should not affect your insurance rates but you should verify this with your agent.

REAL ESTATE
Real estate can be transferred to the living trust by executing a new deed. This deed will show you as the grantor of the property and you in your capacity as trustee as the grantee of the property. Each state has different forms of deeds and the form of deed used is often very

important. It would be advisable to contact an attorney who is familiar with real estate transfers to determine your state's deed requirements.

If your house is subject to a mortgage, the approval of the mortgage company is generally required. Often the mortgage company will ask for a copy of the trust to make certain that you are the owner of all of the assets in the trust and that you will continue to be responsible for future mortgage payments. It is important to contact your fire and casualty insurance company to change the policy to reflect the trust as the new owner of your home.

In some states there is a homestead exemption for real estate taxes on your home. This exemption can result in significant real estate tax savings over the years. Once your homestead property is transferred to your trust, you no longer own the property, the trust does. Trusts generally do not qualify for the homestead exemption. However, many states recognize that the living trust is simply your "alter ego" and will permit the homestead exemption to continue. Prior to transferring your homestead to your trust you should check with the local taxing authorities to make certain that the homestead exemption will continue and what, if any, forms you must complete to protect the homestead exemption.

BANK ACCOUNTS

Checking and savings accounts, and other accounts at financial institutions should be retitled as follows:

`[YOUR NAME], trustee, [YOUR NAME] Trust, dated _____, _____.`

REGISTERED STOCKS AND BONDS

Your stock broker can work with you to re-register the stocks and bonds that you now own. You may need to complete a stock transfer power of attorney and surrender your stock certificates to the broker so he or she can have new certificates issued to your trust. As you acquire stocks in the future, simply have them titled in the name of the trust (as described above).

Bonds should also be re-registered in the name of the trust. Again, your stock broker can assist you with this or you can contact the issuing institution directly to get the appropriate forms.

Sometimes stocks and bonds are held in a "street name" or custodian account with your broker. The broker often collects all interest and dividends on the stocks and bonds and disposes of them according to your instructions, i.e. pays them out directly to you or deposits them into some sort of money market account. These street name accounts can also be registered in the name of the trust.

LIFE INSURANCE
The beneficiary designations on your life insurance policies should be changed to make your trust the beneficiary. The beneficiary designation should read:

```
The Then Acting Trustee of the YOUR NAME Trust, dated
_____, _____.
```

RETIREMENT PLANS
Because of the specific and complex tax rules governing tax qualified retirement plans such as 401(k), pensions, profit-sharing plans, IRAs, Keoghs, etc. you should consult with a tax professional to determine whether your trust should be named as the beneficiary of such plans.

Do not hesitate to contact professionals to assist you with the property transfers. Your stock broker and banker should be willing to help with these transfers with no additional charge to you. Don't let them drag their feet! Keep after them to get the assets transferred.

If you are having trouble with the real estate transfers, or if you own real estate outside of your state of residence, you should contact an attorney who can assist you. The charge for this service should be nominal. Often, the fee paid to an attorney is well worth it because it can save you a lot of frustration and time. More than likely, there will be a recording or document fee that is charged by the county when a new deed is filed. This fee covers the cost of entering the new deed in the county land records. You should not have to pay documentary stamp fees (transfer fees) on a deed to your own trust.

Once you have initially funded your living trust, you must keep separate records for the trust property. As you acquire property in the future, title it directly in the name of the trust. As you sell trust property, keep the proceeds in a special trust bank account. As the grantor of the trust, you can distribute trust property to yourself at any time with little or no additional effort, so there is no reason to allow the proceeds to end up outside the trust. There is much to be gained by keeping the property in the trust so you should take the extra time to make certain that the goal of your living trust, probate avoidance, is met.

Appendix A
Living Trusts and
Related Forms

The following pages contain forms which can be used to prepare a living trust, pourover will, and assign personal property to the trust. The forms should only be used by persons who have read this book, who do not have any complications in their legal affairs, and who understand the forms they are using.

The forms may be used right out of the book or they may be photocopied or retyped. Each form is numbered in the upper right corner. Be sure you have the correct form number. If there is anything you do not understand be sure to consult an attorney.

The following is a list of the forms contained in this appendix, along with the page number where each form begins:

Table of Forms

LAST WILL AND TESTAMENT

OF

_____

I, _____, a resident of

_____ County, State of _____,

do hereby make, publish and declare this to be my Last Will and Testament and revoke any prior

wills and codicils.

FIRST: My Spouse is _____ and my

Children are: _____

_____ and

any other children born to or adopted by me after the date of this Will.

SECOND: I direct that all of my just debts, taxes and funeral expenses be paid out of my

estate as soon after my death as is practical.

THIRD: I give my interest in all of my tangible personal property (including, but not lim-

ited to, my jewelry, clothing, books, china, crystal, silverware, furniture and furnishings, objects of

art, and automobiles), to my spouse. If my spouse is not alive, I give such property to my Children

who survive me in shares of substantially equal value to be divided as they agree. If none of my

Children survive me, I give such property to _____

_____.

FOURTH: I give the rest, remainder and residue of my estate, real and personal, where-

soever situate, now owned or hereafter acquired by me, to the Trustee of my Living Trust, dated

_____, _____, to be added to the trust, subject to its terms as now

provided and as amended from time to time.

FIFTH: If I am the surviving natural parent of my Children, I appoint

_____ as

guardian of the person of each of my minor Children.

SIXTH: I hereby, nominate, constitute and appoint _____

_____to serve as executor of my Last Will and

Testament, to serve without bond or surety. In the event _____

_____is unable or unwilling to serve for any reason, then

I nominate, constitute and appoint _____

_____as alternate executor also to serve without bond or

other surety. I give my executor the fullest power in all matters including the power to sell or convey real or personal property or any interest therein without court order.

IN WITNESS WHEREOF, I have signed and published this my Last Will and Testament this _____ day of _____, _____.

_____

We, the undersigned persons, of lawful age, have on this _____ day of _____, _____, at the request of _____, _____witnessed his/her signature to the foregoing Will in the presence of each of us; and we have, at the same time and in his/her presence and in the presence of each other, subscribed our names hereto as attesting witnesses.

_____   ADDRESS: _____

WITNESS   _____

_____   ADDRESS: _____

WITNESS   _____

_____   ADDRESS: _____

WITNESS   _____

LAST WILL AND TESTAMENT

OF

_____

I,_____, a resident of
_____ County, State of _____, do hereby
make, publish and declare this to be my Last Will and Testament and revoke any prior wills and
codicils.

    FIRST: My Children are: _____
_____and any
other children born to or adopted by me after the date of this Will.

    SECOND: I direct that all of my just debts, taxes and funeral expenses be paid out of my
estate as soon after my death as is practical.

    THIRD: I give my interest in all of my tangible personal property (including, but not limited to, my jewelry, clothing, books, china, crystal, silverware, furniture and furnishings, objects of
art, and automobiles), to my Children who survive me in shares of substantially equal value to be
divided as they agree. If none of my Children survive me, I give such property to
_____.

    FOURTH: I give the rest, remainder and residue of my estate, real and personal, wheresoever situate, now owned or hereafter acquired by me, to the Trustee of my Living Trust, dated
_____, _____, to be added to the trust, subject to its terms as now provided
and as amended from time to time.

    FIFTH: If I am the surviving natural parent of my Children, I appoint
_____
as guardian of the person of each of my minor Children.

    SIXTH: I hereby, nominate, constitute and appoint _____
_____to serve as executor of my Last Will and
Testament, to serve without bond or surety. In the event _____
_____is unable or unwilling to serve for any reason, then I
nominate, constitute and appoint _____
_____as alternate executor also to serve without bond or other
surety. I give my executor the fullest power in all matters including the power to sell or convey
real or personal property or any interest therein without court order.

IN WITNESS WHEREOF, I have signed and published this my Last Will and Testament this _____ day of _____, _____.

_____

We, the undersigned persons, of lawful age, have on this _____ day of _____, _____, at the request of _____, _____witnessed his/her signature to the foregoing Will in the presence of each of us; and we have, at the same time and in his/her presence and in the presence of each other, subscribed our names hereto as attesting witnesses.

_____   ADDRESS: _____

WITNESS   _____

_____   ADDRESS: _____

WITNESS   _____

_____   ADDRESS: _____

WITNESS   _____

ESTATE PLANNING WORKSHEET

I. FAMILY INFORMATION

Date _____

Husband

_____
Name

_____
Address

_____
Phone Number

_____
Birth Date

_____
Employer

_____
Address/Phone Number

Wife

_____
Name

_____
Address

_____
Phone Number

_____
Birth Date

_____
Employer

_____
Address/Phone Number

Children	Birth Date	Social Security Number
1. _____	_____	_____
2. _____	_____	_____
3. _____	_____	_____

Grandchildren/Other dependents	Birth Date	Social Security Number
1. _____	_____	_____
2. _____	_____	_____
3. _____	_____	_____

II. IMPORTANT FAMILY ADVISORS
(include name, address and phone number)

Lawyer _____

Accountant_____

Bank Officer_____

Clergy _____

Doctor_____

Insurance agent_____

Stockbroker_____

III. FINANCIAL INFORMATION

A.   ASSETS

Real estate (land, homes, business property, condos, co-ops, etc.):

Address	Ownership (sole, joint, etc.)	Value/Equity	Mortgage Balance
_____	_____	_____	_____
_____	_____	_____	_____
_____	_____	_____	_____

Cash (checking and savings accounts, money market accounts, CDs, etc.):

Type	Bank	Account Number	Balance
_____	_____	_____	_____
_____	_____	_____	_____
_____	_____	_____	_____

Investments (stocks, bonds, mutual fund shares, etc.):

Description	Company	Number of Shares	Market Value
_____	_____	_____	_____
_____	_____	_____	_____
_____	_____	_____	_____

Personal Property

(only list assets of significant value such as jewelry, antiques, artwork, collectibles, etc.):

Description and Value

_____

_____

_____

Retirement plans (IRAs, 401Ks, pension plans, Keoghs, etc.):

Type	Name of PlanBeneficiary	Current	Value
_____	_____	_____	_____
_____	_____	_____	_____
_____	_____	_____	_____

Life Insurance:

Insured	Company/ Policy Number	Beneficiary	Death Benefit Whole Life or Term
_____	_____	_____	_____
_____	_____	_____	_____
_____	_____	_____	_____

Debts owed to you:

Name and Address of Person who owes you   Amount Owed

_____   _____

_____   _____

_____   _____

B. DEBTS

Type	Company/Person Owed	Amount Owed	When Due	Secured by
Mortgages	_____	_____	_____	_____
Installment Loans	_____	_____	_____	_____
Education loans	_____	_____	_____	_____
Personal loans	_____	_____	_____	_____
Other debts	_____	_____	_____	_____

C. NET WORTH

	Husband	Wife	Joint
ASSETS			
Real estate	_____	_____	_____
Cash	_____	_____	_____
Investments	_____	_____	_____
Personal Property	_____	_____	_____
Retirement plans	_____	_____	_____
Life insurance	_____	_____	_____
Debts owed you	_____	_____	_____
Total assets	_____	_____	_____
DEBTS			
Mortgages	_____	_____	_____
Installment loans	_____	_____	_____
Education loans	_____	_____	_____
Personal loans	_____	_____	_____
Other debts	_____	_____	_____
Total liabilities	_____	_____	_____
NET WORTH	_____	_____	_____
(assets minus debts)			

IV. WILL INFORMATION

Executor(s)   _____

(Include alternates) _____

_____

Guardian(s) for Minor   _____

Children

(Include alternates) _____

_____

_____

Minor Beneficiaries   _____

_____

_____

Other Beneficiaries   _____

_____

_____

Charitable Beneficiaries   _____

_____

_____

Alternate Beneficiaries   _____

_____

_____

V. TRUST INFORMATION

Trustee(s)   _____

(Include alternates)   _____

_____

Minor Beneficiaries   _____

_____

_____

Other Beneficiaries   _____

_____

_____

Charitable Beneficiaries   _____

_____

Alternate Beneficiaries   _____

_____

_____ LIVING TRUST

THIS AGREEMENT OF TRUST is entered into at _____, State of _____, this _____ day of _____, _____, by and between _____, as Grantor and Trustee. This Trust, as from time to time amended, shall be known as the "_____ LIVING TRUST dated _____, _____."

ARTICLE I

My Spouse. My spouse is: _____.

My Children. My Children are: _____

_____.

ARTICLE II

FUNDING

Initial Funding. I hereby transfer to Trustee the sum of Ten Dollars ($10.00).

Additional Funding. From time to time the trust may be funded with additional property by me or by any other person in any manner. All property transferred, assigned, conveyed or delivered to the Trustee shall be held, administered and distributed by the Trustee in accordance with the terms of this Trust Agreement.

ARTICLE III

ADMINISTRATION OF TRUST DURING MY LIFETIME

Distributions of Income. While I am living, the Trustee shall distribute the trust's net income as directed in writing by me from time to time. In default of such direction, the Trustee shall pay to or expend on behalf of me all of the trust's net income from the Trust quarterly or more frequently.

Distributions of Principal. The Trustee shall pay to or expend for my benefit such part or all of the principal of the trust as I may request, from time to time. In default of such direction, the Trustee shall pay to or expend for my benefit so much of the principal of the trust as the Trustee, determines to be necessary or advisable for my health, maintenance and support.

Use of Residential Property. If any real property used by me for residential purposes (whether on a full-time or part-time basis, including recreational property) becomes part of the trust estate, I shall have the right to use and occupy such property without rental or other accounting to the trust estate.

Distributions to My Spouse and Children. The Trustee shall pay to or expend for the benefit of my spouse and minor Children so much of the principal of the trust as the Trustee, in his/her sole discretion, determines to be necessary for the education, health, maintenance and support of my spouse and Children. The Trustee shall make such discretionary distributions only after conferring with me. The trust distributions do not need to be equal.

ARTICLE IV

ADMINISTRATION OF TRUST UPON MY DEATH

Payment of Expenses, Claims and Taxes. Upon my death, the Trustee shall, upon the request of the Executor of my estate, pay such part or all of the expenses of the last illness, funeral, and burial, legally enforceable claims against me or my estate and estate administration expenses. The Trustee may also pay any estate, inheritance, or succession taxes, state, federal and foreign, or any other taxes together with interest and penalties thereon that are payable by reason of my death.

ARTICLE V

DISTRIBUTION OF TRUST TO MY SPOUSE AND CHILDREN

Tangible Personal Property. The Trustee shall distribute my tangible personal property in accordance with any written, signed and dated memorandum prepared by me. Any tangible personal property which is not disposed of by memorandum shall be distributed to my spouse or if my spouse is not alive in equal shares to my surviving Children.

Specific Bequest. The Trustee shall distribute the following property to the named individuals:

_____ to _____

_____ to _____

If any of the individuals named does not survive me, the gift to that person will lapse and the property will pass as provided below.

Distribution to My Spouse. If my spouse survives me, the Trustee shall distribute the remaining trust estate to my spouse outright or, if my spouse so chooses, to the Living Trust dated _____, _____, established by my spouse. If my spouse does not survive me, the Trustee shall distribute the trust estate as provided in the next paragraph.

Distribution to My Children. The Trustee shall divide the remaining trust estate, including any additions to the Trust by reason of my death, into separate equal shares as follows: one share for each Child of mine who is then living, and one share for the then living descendants, collectively, of each deceased Child of mine with one or more descendants then living. The Trustee shall distribute the share for each Child to such Child outright. The share for the descendants of each deceased Child, shall be distributed, per stirpes, to those descendants living at my death.

Contingent Distribution. If my spouse, my Children and their descendants and all of my descendants are deceased, the trust estate then remaining shall be distributed, to the following individuals in the amounts specified:

_____ to_____

_____ to_____

ARTICLE VI

THE TRUSTEE

Successor Trustees. During my lifetime, if I cannot serve as Trustee, I will appoint a successor Trustee. If I do not appoint a successor trustee, or after my death, the successor trustee shall be my spouse, or if my spouse is not able to serve, the successor trustee(s) shall be _____. If the successor trustee fails or ceases to serve, _____ shall be successor trustee. If all successor trustees fail or cease to serve, a majority in number of the income beneficiaries of the trust at that time shall appoint a successor trustee. Any appointment under this section shall be by a signed, acknowledged instrument delivered to the successor trustee.

Removal of Trustee. During my life, I may remove a trustee at any time for any reason. After my death or if I am incapacitated and unable to remove the trustee, my spouse may remove the trustee. If my spouse is not alive or is unable to exercise this power, _____ shall have the power to remove a trustee.

Resignation of Trustee. A Trustee may resign as to any one or more of the trusts created hereunder by giving written notice to all co-trustees then serving, if any, the current income beneficiaries, the successor trustee if identified in this Trust Agreement, and to those persons, if any, authorized in this Trust Agreement to appoint the successor trustee. Notice shall be delivered at least thirty (30) days prior to the date of resignation.

Trustee's Fees. The Trustee shall be entitled to reasonable fees commensurate with the Trustee's duties and responsibilities, taking into account the value and nature of the trust estate and the time and work involved. The Trustee shall be reimbursed for reasonable costs and expenses incurred in connection with fiduciary duties.

Bond. The Trustee shall not be required to furnish bond or other security.

Liability of Trustee. A Trustee shall only be liable for willful misconduct or gross negligence, and shall not be liable for breach of fiduciary duty by virtue of mistake or error in judgment.

Incapacity of Individual Trustee. This Section shall apply in the event a Trustee becomes unable to discharge the duties of Trustee by reason of accident, physical or mental illness or deterioration, or other cause, and does not resign. Upon certification by two medical doctors that each has examined the Trustee and has concluded that the Trustee is unable to discharge such duties, the Trustee shall cease to serve, as if the Trustee had resigned, effective the date of the certification.

ARTICLE VII

TRUST ADMINISTRATION

Trustee Powers: Investment and Management of Trust Estate. Subject to any limitation stated elsewhere in this instrument, the Trustee shall have, with respect to each trust established hereunder, all of the powers granted to trustees by common law and by applicable statutes as amended from time to time. In addition, the trustee shall have the following powers:

(a) **Retain Property.** To retain any property received from any source, regardless of lack of diversification, risk, or nonproductivity.

(b) **Invest.** To invest the trust estate in any kind of property, without being limited by any law dealing with the character, risk, productivity, diversification, wasting nature of, or otherwise concerning, investments by trustees.

(c) **Sell.** By public offering or private negotiation, to sell, exchange, assign, transfer, or otherwise dispose of all or any real or personal trust property and give options for these purposes, for such price and on such terms, with such covenants of warranty and such security for deferred payment as the Trustee deems proper. To partition between the trust and any other owner, as the Trustee deems proper, any property in which the trust owns an undivided interest.

(d) **Lease.** To lease trust property for terms within or extending beyond the term of the trust, for any purpose.

(e) **Real Estate.** To operate, maintain, repair, rehabilitate, alter, erect, improve, or remove any improvements on real estate; to subdivide real estate; to grant easements, give consents, and enter into contracts relating to real estate or its use; and to release or dedicate any interest in real estate.

(f) **Borrow.** To borrow money for any purpose; to encumber or hypothecate trust property by mortgage, deed of trust, or otherwise; and to maintain, prepay, renew, or extend any indebtedness upon such terms as the Trustee deems appropriate.

(g) **Loans.** To lend money to any person or entity, including, but not limited to, a beneficiary hereunder, upon such terms and with such security as the Trustee deems advisable.

(h) **Securities.** To engage in all actions necessary to the effective administration of securities including, but not limited to, the authority to: vote securities in person or by proxy; engage in a voting trust or voting agreement; exercise any options, rights, or privileges pertaining to any trust property; and consent to or participate in mergers, consolidations, sales of assets, recapitalizations, reorganizations, dissolutions, or other alterations of corporate structure affecting securities held by the Trustee.

(i) **Business Powers.** To enter into, carry on, and expand or acquire additional interests in (through the investment or loan of trust funds) any business activity, in sole proprietorship, general or limited partnership, joint venture, corporate or other form (and to convert from one form to another), including, but not limited to, any business interest which may be contributed to the trust, to employ agents and confer upon them the authority to manage and operate such business activity without liability for the acts of any such agents or for any loss, liability or indebtedness of such business, if the agents are selected and retained with reasonable care; and to sell, liquidate, or otherwise terminate any business interest, including, but not limited to, the fulfillment of any agreement for the disposition of any such business interest.

(j) **Litigation.** To commence or defend at the expense of the trust such litigation with respect to the trust estate as the Trustee deems advisable.

(k) **Claims.** To collect, pay, contest, compromise, settle, renew, or abandon any claims or demands of or against the trust estate, on whatever terms the Trustee deems advisable.

(l) **Additional Property.** To receive from any source additional property which is acceptable to the Trustee, and add it to the trust estate.

(m) **Agents.** To employ attorneys, auditors, brokers, investment advisors, depositaries, and agents with or without discretionary powers, to employ a trust company or bank with trust powers as agent for the purpose of performing any delegable duties of the administration, and to pay all expenses and fees so incurred.

(n) **Nominee.** To hold securities and other property in bearer form or in the name of a Trustee or nominee with or without disclosure of any fiduciary relationship.

(o) **Miscellaneous Powers.** Generally, to do and perform any and all acts, things, or deeds which an individual could do with respect to property and which, in the judgment of the Trustee, may be necessary or proper for the investment, management, protection and promotion of the property of the trust estate.

(p) **Tax Elections.** Unless otherwise expressly directed hereunder, to exercise any tax option, allocation or election permitted by law as the Trustee determines in the Trustee's sole discretion.

(q) **Division and Distribution.** To make all allocations, distributions, or divisions contemplated by this instrument; to allocate, distribute and divide different kinds or disproportionate shares of property or undivided interests in property among the beneficiaries or trusts, in cash or in kind, or both, without regard to the income tax basis of specific property allocated to any beneficiary or trust, even though shares may as a result be composed differently, and to determine the value of any property so allocated, divided or distributed.

(r) **Reliance.** To rely upon any notice, certificate, affidavit, or other document or evidence believed by the Trustee to be genuine and accurate, in making any payment or distribution. The Trustee shall incur no liability for a disbursement or distribution made in good faith and without actual notice or knowledge of a changed condition or status affecting any person's interest in the trust or any other matter.

Court Supervision. The Trustee shall not be required to qualify before or be appointed by any court; nor shall the Trustee be required to obtain the order or approval of any court in the exercise of any power or discretion.

Periodic Accounting. The Trustee shall make reports at least annually to those beneficiaries who may receive current distributions, such reports to reflect the property held in trust, the receipts, disbursements, and distributions made during the accounting period, and such other information as may be necessary to convey the condition of and changes to the trust estate.

Beneficiary Under Disability. Where a beneficiary is under the disability of minority or, in the Trustee's opinion, any other legal, physical or mental disability, a parent, custodian or guardian who, entirely in the Trustee's discretion, is acceptable to the Trustee may, in carrying out the provisions of this Trust Agreement, act and receive notice in the beneficiary's place, and sign any instrument for the beneficiary.

Spendthrift Trusts. All trusts created under this Trust Agreement are spendthrift trusts. No beneficiary may anticipate, by assignment or otherwise, a beneficial interest in the principal or income of the trusts created hereunder; nor may any beneficiary sell, transfer, encumber, or in any way charge an interest in trust income or principal prior to actually receiving it. Neither the income nor the principal of any trust established hereunder shall be subject to any execution, garnishment, attachment, bankruptcy, claims for alimony or support, other legal proceeding of any character, legal sequestration, levy or sale, or in any other event or manner be applicable or subject, voluntarily or involuntarily, to the payment of a beneficiary's debts. The Trustee shall make distributions to or for each beneficiary according to the terms hereof, notwithstanding any purported sale, assignment, hypothecation, transfer, attachment, or judicial process.

Limitation on Distributions.

(a) **Support Obligation.** Any other provision of this Trust Agreement notwithstanding, no distribution shall be made which discharges, in whole or in part, the Trustee's legal obligations, from time to time existing, to support, educate or otherwise provide for any of the trust beneficiaries. When determining these legal obligations, the existence of the trust estate and funds made available by it shall not be taken into consideration.

(b) **Distribution to Trustee/Beneficiary.** Notwithstanding anything to the contrary in this Trust Agreement, no Trustee shall have the authority to make discretionary distributions to that person as beneficiary, except to the extent the distributions are for the beneficiary's health, maintenance, support or education. If the Trustee is otherwise in this Trust Agreement authorized to make a distribution beyond that standard, the distributions shall be so limited.

Rule Against Perpetuities. Every trust created hereunder (or through the exercise of a power of appointment granted in this Trust Agreement) must vest not later than twenty-one (21) years after my death and descendants living at the time the trust created hereunder first becomes irrevocable. If a trust is not vested within that period, it will terminate as of the maximum vesting date. In the event of termination, the Trustee shall distribute each trust to its income beneficiaries determined at the time of distribution in the proportions to which they are entitled to receive income.

Out-of-State Properties. If the Trustee must act in a jurisdiction in which a person or entity serving as Trustee is unable or unwilling to act, the other or others serving as Trustee may act in that jurisdiction. If no Trustee is able or willing to act, the Trustee may appoint an ancillary trustee for that jurisdiction and may confer upon the ancillary trustee such rights, powers, discretions and duties, exercisable without court order, to act with respect to such matters as the Trustee deems proper. The ancillary trustee shall be responsible to the Trustee for any property it administers. The Trustee may pay the ancillary trustee reasonable compensation for services and may absolve the ancillary trustee from any requirement to furnish bond or other security.

ARTICLE VIII

AMENDMENT AND REVOCATION OF TRUST

I may amend, revoke or modify this Trust Agreement in whole or in part by an instrument signed and acknowledged by me and delivered to the Trustee. Amendment or modification of the Trust Agreement shall be effective immediately upon delivery of the instrument to the Trustee, except that changes affecting the Trustee's duties, liabilities, or compensation shall not be effective without the Trustee's written consent. On my death, this Trust Agreement may no longer be amended or modified, and the trust created hereunder shall become irrevocable.

ARTICLE IX

MISCELLANEOUS PROVISIONS

Applicable Law. The validity, construction, and administration of each trust created hereunder shall be governed by the laws of the State of _____.

Adoption. For purposes of this Trust Agreement, a person shall be regarded as having been legally adopted by another only if the adoption is by court proceedings, the finality of which is not being contested by the adopting person.

Survival. Any person must survive by thirty (30) days for a gift made in this Trust Agreement which directly or indirectly requires such person's survival of another to be effective.

Education. "Education" shall include preparatory, collegiate, postgraduate, professional and vocational education; specialized formal or informal training in music, the stage, handicrafts, the arts or sports or athletic endeavors, whether by private instruction or otherwise; and any other activity, including foreign or domestic travel, which tends to develop the talents and potential of the beneficiary, regardless of age. Education shall also include all tuition, board, lodging fees, books and equipment, travel expenses and other expenses incidental thereto.

Executor. "Executor" shall include personal representative, executrix, administrator and administratrix.

Health. "Health" shall include medical, dental, hospital and nursing care expenses, and other expenses of invalidism, and distributions for the "health" of a beneficiary may, in the discretion of the Trustee include any part or all of the costs of purchasing or maintaining hospital or medical insurance and disability income insurance coverage for such beneficiary and/or any person in whom such beneficiary has an insurable interest.

Binding Agreement. This agreement shall extend to and be binding upon the heirs, executors, administrators, successors and assigns of the parties.

Use of Words. As used in this instrument, the masculine, feminine, and neuter gender, and the singular or plural of any word includes the others unless the context indicates otherwise.

Unenforceable Provision. If any provision of this Trust Agreement is unenforceable, the remaining provisions shall be given effect, unless to do so would produce an unreasonable result.

Titles, Headings, and Captions. All titles, headings, and captions used in this Trust Agreement have been included for convenience only and should not be construed in interpreting this instrument.

IN WITNESS WHEREOF, I as Grantor and Trustee have hereunto set my hand, on the day and year first above written in multiple originals.

_____   _____
Witness   Grantor

_____   _____
Witness   Trustee

STATE OF _____ §
                                 §
COUNTY OF _____ §

BEFORE ME, the undersigned authority, on this day personally appeared _____, Grantor and Trustee, known to me to be the person whose name is subscribed to the foregoing instrument and acknowledged to me that he/she executed the same for the purposes and consideration therein expressed.

GIVEN UNDER MY HAND AND SEAL OF OFFICE this _____ day of _____, _____.

                                           _____
                                           Notary Public
                                           My Commission Expires:

_____ LIVING TRUST

THIS AGREEMENT OF TRUST is entered into at _____, State of _____, this _____ day of _____, _____, by and between _____, as Grantor and Trustee. This Trust, as from time to time amended, shall be known as the "_____ LIVING TRUST dated _____, _____."

ARTICLE I

My Spouse. My Spouse is: _____.

My Children. My Children are: _____

_____ .

ARTICLE II

FUNDING

Initial Funding. I hereby transfer to Trustee the sum of Ten Dollars ($10.00).

Additional Funding. From time to time the trust may be funded with additional property by me or by any other person in any manner. All property transferred, assigned, conveyed or delivered to the Trustee shall be held, administered and distributed by the Trustee in accordance with the terms of this Trust Agreement.

ARTICLE III

ADMINISTRATION OF TRUST DURING MY LIFETIME

Distributions of Income. While I am living, the Trustee shall distribute the trust's net income as directed in writing by me from time to time. In default of such direction, the Trustee shall pay to or expend on behalf of me all of the trust's net income from the Trust quarterly or more frequently.

Distributions of Principal. The Trustee shall pay to or expend for my benefit such part or all of the principal of the trust as I may request, from time to time. In default of such direction, the Trustee shall pay to or expend for my benefit so much of the principal of the trust as the Trustee, determines to be necessary or advisable for my health, maintenance and support.

Use of Residential Property. If any real property used by me for residential purposes (whether on a full-time or part-time basis, including recreational property) becomes part of the trust estate, I shall have the right to use and occupy such property without rental or other accounting to the trust estate.

Distributions to My Spouse and Children. The Trustee shall pay to or expend for the benefit of my spouse and minor Children so much of the principal of the trust as the Trustee, in his/her sole discretion, determines to be necessary for the education, health, maintenance and support of my spouse and Children. The Trustee shall make such discretionary distributions only after conferring with me. The trust distributions do not need to be equal.

ARTICLE IV

ADMINISTRATION OF TRUST UPON MY DEATH

Payment of Expenses, Claims and Taxes. Upon my death, the Trustee shall, upon the request of the Executor of my estate, pay such part or all of the expenses of the last illness, funeral, and burial, legally enforceable claims against me or my estate and estate administration expenses. The Trustee may also pay any estate, inheritance, or succession taxes, state, federal and foreign, or any other taxes together with interest and penalties thereon that are payable by reason of my death.

ARTICLE V

DISTRIBUTIONS OF TRUST TO MY SPOUSE AND CHILDREN

Tangible Personal Property. The Trustee shall distribute my tangible personal property in accordance with any written, signed and dated memorandum prepared by me. Any tangible personal property which is not disposed of by memorandum shall be distributed to my spouse or if my spouse is not alive in equal shares to my surviving Children.

Specific Bequest. The Trustee shall distribute the following property to the named individuals:

_____ to _____

_____ to _____

If any of the individuals named does not survive me, the gift to that person will lapse and the property will pass as provided below.

Distribution to My Spouse. If my spouse survives me, the Trustee shall distribute the remaining trust estate to my spouse outright or, if my spouse so chooses, to the Living Trust dated _____, _____, established by my spouse. If my spouse does not survive me, the Trustee shall distribute the trust estate as provided in the next paragraph.

Division of Trust Estate for My Children. The Trustee shall divide the remaining trust estate, including any additions to the Trust by reason of my death, into separate equal shares as follows: one share for each Child of mine who is then living, and one share for the then living descendants, collectively, of each deceased Child of mine with one or more descendants then living. The Trustee shall administer a share for each Child in a separate trust, and a share for the Descendants of each deceased Child, pursuant to the provisions of Article VI, following.

ARTICLE VI

TRUSTS FOR CHILDREN AND DESCENDANTS

Separate Trust for Child. Each trust for the benefit of a Child shall be administered and distributed upon the following terms:

(a) **Distributions to Child.** The Trustee shall distribute to the Child all of the trust's net income quarterly or more frequently and so much of the principal of the trust as the Trustee deems necessary to provide for the Child's health, maintenance, education and support.

When the Child attains age _____, the Trustee shall distribute to the Child _____ of the value of the then remaining trust estate.

When the Child attains age _____, the Trustee shall distribute to the Child the remaining trust estate.

(b) **Termination of Trust.** If not earlier terminated by distribution of the entire trust estate under the foregoing provisions, the trust shall terminate upon the death of the Child. The Trustee shall distribute the remaining trust estate to the Child's then living descendants, pursuant to the limitation described in subsection (c) hereof. If there are no descendants of the Child then living, the Trustee shall distribute the remaining trust estate to my then living descendants, per stirpes.

(c) **Distribution to Descendants of a Deceased Child.** Property which is to be distributed under this subsection to the descendants of a deceased Child shall be distributed, per stirpes, to those descendants living at the event causing the distribution hereunder.

Contingent Distribution. If my spouse, my Children and their descendants and all of my descendants are deceased, the trust estate then remaining shall be distributed, to the following individuals in the amounts specified:

_____ to_____

_____ to_____

ARTICLE VII

THE TRUSTEE

Successor Trustees. During my lifetime, if I cannot serve as Trustee, I will appoint a successor Trustee. If I do not appoint a successor trustee, or after my death, the successor trustee shall be my spouse, or if I am not married or my spouse is not able to serve, the successor trustee(s) shall be:_____. If the successor trustee fails or ceases to serve, _____ shall be successor trustee. If all successor trustees fail or cease to serve, a majority in number of the income beneficiaries of the trust at that time shall appoint a successor trustee.

Any appointment under this Section shall be by a signed, acknowledged instrument delivered to the successor trustee.

Removal of Trustee. During my life, I may remove a trustee at any time for any reason. After my death or if I am incapacitated and unable to remove the trustee, my spouse may remove the trustee. If my spouse is not alive or is unable to exercise this power, _____ _____ shall have the power to remove a trustee.

Resignation of Trustee. A Trustee may resign as to any one or more of the trusts created hereunder by giving written notice to all co-trustees then serving, if any, the current income beneficiaries, the successor trustee if identified in this Trust Agreement, and to those persons, if any, authorized in this Trust Agreement to appoint the successor trustee. Notice shall be delivered at least thirty (30) days prior to the date of resignation.

Trustee's Fees. The Trustee shall be entitled to reasonable fees commensurate with the Trustee's duties and responsibilities, taking into account the value and nature of the trust estate and the time and work involved. The Trustee shall be reimbursed for reasonable costs and expenses incurred in connection with fiduciary duties.

Bond. The Trustee shall not be required to furnish bond or other security.

Liability of Trustee. A Trustee shall only be liable for willful misconduct or gross negligence, and shall not be liable for breach of fiduciary duty by virtue of mistake or error in judgment.

Incapacity of Individual Trustee. This Section shall apply in the event a Trustee becomes unable to discharge the duties of Trustee by reason of accident, physical or mental illness or deterioration, or other cause, and does not resign. Upon certification by two medical doctors that each has examined the Trustee and has concluded that the Trustee is unable to discharge such duties, the Trustee shall cease to serve, as if the Trustee had resigned, effective the date of the certification.

ARTICLE VIII

TRUST ADMINISTRATION

Trustee Powers: Investment and Management of Trust Estate. Subject to any limitation stated elsewhere in this instrument, the Trustee shall have, with respect to each trust established hereunder, all of the powers granted to trustees by common law and by applicable statutes as amended from time to time. In addition, the trustee shall have the following powers:

(a) **Retain Property.** To retain any property received from any source, regardless of lack of diversification, risk, or nonproductivity.

(b) **Invest.** To invest the trust estate in any kind of property, without being limited by any law dealing with the character, risk, productivity, diversification, wasting nature of, or otherwise concerning, investments by trustees.

(c) **Sell.** By public offering or private negotiation, to sell, exchange, assign, transfer, or otherwise dispose of all or any real or personal trust property and give options for these purposes, for such price and on such terms, with such covenants of warranty and such security for deferred payment as the Trustee deems proper. To partition between the trust and any other owner, as the Trustee deems proper, any property in which the trust owns an undivided interest.

(d) **Lease.** To lease trust property for terms within or extending beyond the term of the trust, for any purpose.

(e) **Real Estate.** To operate, maintain, repair, rehabilitate, alter, erect, improve, or remove any improvements on real estate; to subdivide real estate; to grant easements, give consents, and enter into contracts relating to real estate or its use; and to release or dedicate any interest in real estate.

(f) **Borrow.** To borrow money for any purpose; to encumber or hypothecate trust property by mortgage, deed of trust, or otherwise; and to maintain, prepay, renew, or extend any indebtedness upon such terms as the Trustee deems appropriate.

(g) **Loans.** To lend money to any person or entity, including, but not limited to, a beneficiary hereunder, upon such terms and with such security as the Trustee deems advisable.

(h) **Securities.** To engage in all actions necessary to the effective administration of securities including, but not limited to, the authority to: vote securities in person or by proxy; engage in a voting trust or voting agreement; exercise any options, rights, or privileges pertaining to any trust property; and consent to or participate in mergers, consolidations, sales of assets, recapitalizations, reorganizations, dissolutions, or other alterations of corporate structure affecting securities held by the Trustee.

(i) **Business Powers.** To enter into, carry on, and expand or acquire additional interests in (through the investment or loan of trust funds) any business activity, in sole proprietorship, general or limited partnership, joint venture, corporate or other form (and to convert from one form to another), including, but not limited to, any business interest which may be contributed to the trust, to employ agents and confer upon them the authority to manage and operate such business activity without liability for the acts of any such agents or for any loss, liability or indebtedness of such business, if the agents are selected and retained with reasonable care; and to sell, liquidate, or otherwise terminate any business interest, including, but not limited to, the fulfillment of any agreement for the disposition of any such business interest.

(j) **Litigation.** To commence or defend at the expense of the trust such litigation with respect to the trust estate as the Trustee deems advisable.

(k) **Claims.** To collect, pay, contest, compromise, settle, renew, or abandon any claims or demands of or against the trust estate, on whatever terms the Trustee deems advisable.

(l) **Additional Property.** To receive from any source additional property which is acceptable to the Trustee, and add it to the trust estate.

(m) **Agents.** To employ attorneys, auditors, brokers, investment advisors, depositaries, and agents with or without discretionary powers, to employ a trust company or bank with trust powers as agent for the purpose of performing any delegable duties of the administration, and to pay all expenses and fees so incurred.

(n) **Nominee.** To hold securities and other property in bearer form or in the name of a Trustee or nominee with or without disclosure of any fiduciary relationship.

(o) **Miscellaneous Powers.** Generally, to do and perform any and all acts, things, or deeds which an individual could do with respect to property and which, in the judgment of the Trustee, may be necessary or proper for the investment, management, protection and promotion of the property of the trust estate.

(p) **Tax Elections.** Unless otherwise expressly directed hereunder, to exercise any tax option, allocation or election permitted by law as the Trustee determines in the Trustee's sole discretion.

(q) **Division and Distribution.** To make all allocations, distributions, or divisions contemplated by this instrument; to allocate, distribute and divide different kinds or disproportionate shares of property or undivided interests in property among the beneficiaries or trusts, in cash or in kind, or both, without regard to the income tax basis of specific property allocated to any beneficiary or trust, even though shares may as a result be composed differently, and to determine the value of any property so allocated, divided or distributed.

(r) **Reliance.** To rely upon any notice, certificate, affidavit, or other document or evidence believed by the Trustee to be genuine and accurate, in making any payment or distribution. The Trustee shall incur no liability for a disbursement or distribution made in good faith and without actual notice or knowledge of a changed condition or status affecting any person's interest in the trust or any other matter.

Court Supervision. The Trustee shall not be required to qualify before or be appointed by any court; nor shall the Trustee be required to obtain the order or approval of any court in the exercise of any power or discretion.

Periodic Accounting. The Trustee shall make reports at least annually to those beneficiaries who may receive current distributions, such reports to reflect the property held in trust, the receipts, disbursements, and distributions made during the accounting period, and such other information as may be necessary to convey the condition of and changes to the trust estate.

Beneficiary Under Disability. Where a beneficiary is under the disability of minority or, in the Trustee's opinion, any other legal, physical or mental disability, a parent, custodian or guardian who, entirely in the Trustee's discretion, is acceptable to the Trustee may, in carrying out the provisions of this Trust Agreement, act and receive notice in the beneficiary's place, and sign any instrument for the beneficiary.

Spendthrift Trusts. All trusts created under this Trust Agreement are spendthrift trusts. No beneficiary may anticipate, by assignment or otherwise, a beneficial interest in the principal or income of the trusts created hereunder; nor may any beneficiary sell, transfer, encumber, or in any way charge an interest in trust income or principal prior to actually receiving it. Neither the income nor the principal of any trust established hereunder shall be subject to any execution, garnishment, attachment, bankruptcy, claims for alimony or support, other legal proceeding of any character, legal sequestration, levy or sale, or in any other event or manner be applicable or subject, voluntarily or involuntarily, to the payment of a beneficiary's debts. The Trustee shall make distributions to or for each beneficiary according to the terms hereof, notwithstanding any purported sale, assignment, hypothecation, transfer, attachment, or judicial process.

Limitation on Distributions.

(a) **Support Obligation.** Any other provision of this Trust Agreement notwithstanding, no distribution shall be made which discharges, in whole or in part, the Trustee's legal obligations, from time to time existing, to support, educate or otherwise provide for any of the trust beneficiaries. When determining these legal obligations, the existence of the trust estate and funds made available by it shall not be taken into consideration.

(b) **Distribution to Trustee/Beneficiary.** Notwithstanding anything to the contrary in this Trust Agreement, no Trustee shall have the authority to make discretionary distributions to that person as beneficiary, except to the extent the distributions are for the beneficiary's health, maintenance, support or education. If the Trustee is otherwise in this Trust Agreement authorized to make a distribution beyond that standard, the distributions shall be so limited.

Rule Against Perpetuities. Every trust created hereunder (or through the exercise of a power of appointment granted in this Trust Agreement) must vest not later than twenty-one (21) years after my death and descendants living at the time the trust created hereunder first becomes irrevocable. If a trust is not vested within that period, it will terminate as of the maximum vesting date. In the event of termination, the Trustee shall distribute each trust to its income beneficiaries determined at the time of distribution in the proportions to which they are entitled to receive income.

Out-of-State Properties. If the Trustee must act in a jurisdiction in which a person or entity serving as Trustee is unable or unwilling to act, the other or others serving as Trustee may act in that jurisdiction. If no Trustee is able or willing to act, the Trustee may appoint an ancillary trustee for that jurisdiction and may confer upon the ancillary trustee such rights, powers, discretions and duties, exercisable without court order, to act with respect to such matters as the Trustee deems proper. The ancillary trustee shall be responsible to the Trustee for any property it administers. The Trustee may pay the ancillary trustee reasonable compensation for services and may absolve the ancillary trustee from any requirement to furnish bond or other security.

ARTICLE IX

AMENDMENT AND REVOCATION OF TRUST

I may amend, revoke or modify this Trust Agreement in whole or in part by an instrument signed and acknowledged by me and delivered to the Trustee. Amendment or modification of the Trust Agreement shall be effective immediately upon delivery of the instrument to the Trustee, except that changes affecting the Trustee's duties, liabilities, or compensation shall not be effective without the Trustee's written consent. On my death, this Trust Agreement may no longer be amended or modified, and the trust created hereunder shall become irrevocable.

ARTICLE X

MISCELLANEOUS PROVISIONS

Applicable Law. The validity, construction, and administration of each trust created hereunder shall be governed by the laws of the State of _____.

Adoption. For purposes of this Trust Agreement, a person shall be regarded as having been legally adopted by another only if the adoption is by court proceedings, the finality of which is not being contested by the adopting person.

Survival. Any person must survive by thirty (30) days for a gift made in this Trust Agreement which directly or indirectly requires such person's survival of another to be effective.

Education. "Education" shall include preparatory, collegiate, postgraduate, professional and vocational education; specialized formal or informal training in music, the stage, handicrafts, the arts or sports or athletic endeavors, whether by private instruction or otherwise; and any other activity, including foreign or domestic travel, which tends to develop the talents and potential of the beneficiary, regardless of age. Education shall also include all tuition, board, lodging fees, books and equipment, travel expenses and other expenses incidental thereto.

Executor. "Executor" shall include personal representative, executrix, administrator and administratrix.

Health. "Health" shall include medical, dental, hospital and nursing care expenses, and other expenses of invalidism, and distributions for the "health" of a beneficiary may, in the discretion of the Trustee include any part or all of the costs of purchasing or maintaining hospital or medical insurance and disability income insurance coverage for such beneficiary and/or any person in whom such beneficiary has an insurable interest.

Binding Agreement. This agreement shall extend to and be binding upon the heirs, executors, administrators, successors and assigns of the parties.

Use of Words. As used in this instrument, the masculine, feminine, and neuter gender, and the singular or plural of any word includes the others unless the context indicates otherwise.

Unenforceable Provision. If any provision of this Trust Agreement is unenforceable, the remaining provisions shall be given effect, unless to do so would produce an unreasonable result.

Titles, Headings, and Captions. All titles, headings, and captions used in this Trust Agreement have been included for convenience only and should not be construed in interpreting this instrument.

IN WITNESS WHEREOF, I as Grantor and Trustee have hereunto set my hand, on the day and year first above written in multiple originals.

_____   _____
Witness   Grantor

_____   _____
Witness   Trustee

STATE OF _____ §
                                §
COUNTY OF _____ §

BEFORE ME, the undersigned authority, on this day personally appeared _____, Grantor and Trustee, known to me to be the person whose name is subscribed to the foregoing instrument and acknowledged to me that he/she executed the same for the purposes and consideration therein expressed.

GIVEN UNDER MY HAND AND SEAL OF OFFICE this ____ day of _____, _____.

                                          _____
                                          Notary Public
                                          My Commission Expires:

_____ LIVING TRUST

THIS AGREEMENT OF TRUST is entered into at _____, State of _____, this _____ day of _____, _____, by and between _____, as Grantor and Trustee. This Trust, as from time to time amended, shall be known as the "_____ LIVING TRUST dated _____, _____."

ARTICLE I

My Children. My Children are: _____ .

ARTICLE II

FUNDING

Initial Funding. I hereby transfer to Trustee the sum of Ten Dollars ($10.00).

Additional Funding. From time to time the trust may be funded with additional property by me or by any other person in any manner. All property transferred, assigned, conveyed or delivered to the Trustee shall be held, administered and distributed by the Trustee in accordance with the terms of this Trust Agreement.

ARTICLE III

ADMINISTRATION OF TRUST DURING MY LIFETIME

Distributions of Income. While I am living, the Trustee shall distribute the trust's net income as directed in writing by me from time to time. In default of such direction, the Trustee shall pay to or expend on behalf of me all of the trust's net income from the Trust quarterly or more frequently.

Distributions of Principal. The Trustee shall pay to or expend for my benefit such part or all of the principal of the trust as I may request, from time to time. In default of such direction, the Trustee shall pay to or expend for my benefit so much of the principal of the trust as the Trustee, determines to be necessary or advisable for my health, maintenance and support.

Use of Residential Property. If any real property used by me for residential purposes (whether on a full-time or part-time basis, including recreational property) becomes part of the trust estate, I shall have the right to use and occupy such property without rental or other accounting to the trust estate.

Distributions to My Children. The Trustee shall pay to or expend for the benefit of my minor children so much of the principal of the trust as the Trustee, in his/her sole discretion, determines to be necessary for the education, health, maintenance and support of my children. The Trustee shall make such discretionary distributions only after conferring with me. The trust distributions do not need to be equal.

ARTICLE IV

ADMINISTRATION OF TRUST UPON MY DEATH

Payment of Expenses, Claims and Taxes. Upon my death, the Trustee shall, upon the request of the Executor of my estate, pay such part or all of the expenses of the last illness, funeral, and burial, legally enforceable claims against me or my estate and estate administration expenses. The Trustee may also pay any estate, inheritance, or succession taxes, state, federal and foreign, or any other taxes together with interest and penalties thereon that are payable by reason of my death.

ARTICLE V

DISTRIBUTION OF TRUST TO MY CHILDREN

Tangible Personal Property. The Trustee shall distribute my tangible personal property in accordance with any written, signed and dated memorandum prepared by me. Any tangible personal property which is not disposed of by memorandum shall be distributed in equal shares to my surviving Children.

Specific Bequest. The Trustee shall distribute the following property to the named individuals:

_____ to _____

_____ to _____

If any of the individuals named does not survive me, the gift to that person will lapse and the property will pass as provided below.

Distribution to My Children. The Trustee shall divide the remaining trust estate, including any additions to the Trust by reason of my death, into separate equal shares as follows: one share for each Child of mine who is then living, and one share for the then living descendants, collectively, of each deceased Child of mine with one or more descendants then living. The Trustee shall distribute the share for each Child to such Child outright. The share for the descendants of each deceased Child, shall be distributed, per stirpes, to those descendants living at the my death.

Contingent Distribution. If my Children and their descendants and all of my descendants are deceased, the trust estate then remaining shall be distributed, to the following individuals in the amounts specified:

_____ to_____

_____ to_____

ARTICLE VI

THE TRUSTEE

Successor Trustees. During my lifetime, if I cannot serve as Trustee, I will appoint a successor Trustee. If I do not appoint a successor trustee, or after my death, the successor trustee shall be _____. If _____ is not able to serve, the successor trustee(s) shall be _____. If the successor trustee fails or ceases to serve, _____ shall be successor trustee. If all successor trustees fail or cease to serve, a majority in number of the income beneficiaries of the trust at that time shall appoint a successor trustee. Any appointment under this section shall be by a signed, acknowledged instrument delivered to the successor trustee.

Removal of Trustee. During my life, I may remove a trustee at any time for any reason. After my death or if I am incapacitated and unable to remove the trustee, _____ _____ may remove the trustee. If _____ is not alive or is unable to exercise this power, _____ _____ shall have the power to remove a trustee.

Resignation of Trustee. A Trustee may resign as to any one or more of the trusts created hereunder by giving written notice to all co-trustees then serving, if any, the current income beneficiaries, the successor trustee if identified in this Trust Agreement, and to those persons, if any, authorized in this Trust Agreement to appoint the successor trustee. Notice shall be delivered at least thirty (30) days prior to the date of resignation.

Trustee's Fees. The Trustee shall be entitled to reasonable fees commensurate with the Trustee's duties and responsibilities, taking into account the value and nature of the trust estate and the time and work involved. The Trustee shall be reimbursed for reasonable costs and expenses incurred in connection with fiduciary duties.

Bond. The Trustee shall not be required to furnish bond or other security.

Liability of Trustee. A Trustee shall only be liable for willful misconduct or gross negligence, and shall not be liable for breach of fiduciary duty by virtue of mistake or error in judgment.

Incapacity of Individual Trustee. This Section shall apply in the event a Trustee becomes unable to discharge the duties of Trustee by reason of accident, physical or mental illness or deterioration, or other cause, and does not resign. Upon certification by two medical doctors that each has examined the Trustee and has concluded that the Trustee is unable to discharge such duties, the Trustee shall cease to serve, as if the Trustee had resigned, effective the date of the certification.

ARTICLE VII

TRUST ADMINISTRATION

Trustee Powers: Investment and Management of Trust Estate. Subject to any limitation stated elsewhere in this instrument, the Trustee shall have, with respect to each trust established hereunder, all of the powers granted to trustees by common law and by applicable statutes as amended from time to time. In addition, the trustee shall have the following powers:

(a) **Retain Property.** To retain any property received from any source, regardless of lack of diversification, risk, or nonproductivity.

(b) **Invest.** To invest the trust estate in any kind of property, without being limited by any law dealing with the character, risk, productivity, diversification, wasting nature of, or otherwise concerning, investments by trustees.

(c) **Sell.** By public offering or private negotiation, to sell, exchange, assign, transfer, or otherwise dispose of all or any real or personal trust property and give options for these purposes, for such price and on such terms, with such covenants of warranty and such security for deferred payment as the Trustee deems proper. To partition between the trust and any other owner, as the Trustee deems proper, any property in which the trust owns an undivided interest.

(d) **Lease.** To lease trust property for terms within or extending beyond the term of the trust, for any purpose.

(e) **Real Estate.** To operate, maintain, repair, rehabilitate, alter, erect, improve, or remove any improvements on real estate; to subdivide real estate; to grant easements, give consents, and enter into contracts relating to real estate or its use; and to release or dedicate any interest in real estate.

(f) **Borrow.** To borrow money for any purpose; to encumber or hypothecate trust property by mortgage, deed of trust, or otherwise; and to maintain, prepay, renew, or extend any indebtedness upon such terms as the Trustee deems appropriate.

(g) **Loans.** To lend money to any person or entity, including, but not limited to, a beneficiary hereunder, upon such terms and with such security as the Trustee deems advisable.

(h) **Securities.** To engage in all actions necessary to the effective administration of securities including, but not limited to, the authority to: vote securities in person or by proxy; engage in a voting trust or voting agreement; exercise any options, rights, or privileges pertaining to any trust property; and consent to or participate in mergers, consolidations, sales of assets, recapitalizations, reorganizations, dissolutions, or other alterations of corporate structure affecting securities held by the Trustee.

(i) **Business Powers.** To enter into, carry on, and expand or acquire additional interests in (through the investment or loan of trust funds) any business activity, in sole proprietorship, general or limited partnership, joint venture, corporate or other form (and to convert from one form to another), including, but not limited to, any business interest which may be contributed to the trust, to employ agents and confer upon them the authority to manage and operate such business activity without liability for the acts of any such agents or for any loss, liability or indebtedness of such business, if the agents are selected and retained with reasonable care; and to sell, liquidate, or otherwise terminate any business interest, including, but not limited to, the fulfillment of any agreement for the disposition of any such business interest.

(j) **Litigation.** To commence or defend at the expense of the trust such litigation with respect to the trust estate as the Trustee deems advisable.

(k) **Claims.** To collect, pay, contest, compromise, settle, renew, or abandon any claims or demands of or against the trust estate, on whatever terms the Trustee deems advisable.

(l) **Additional Property.** To receive from any source additional property which is acceptable to the Trustee, and add it to the trust estate.

(m) **Agents.** To employ attorneys, auditors, brokers, investment advisors, depositaries, and agents with or without discretionary powers, to employ a trust company or bank with trust powers as agent for the purpose of performing any delegable duties of the administration, and to pay all expenses and fees so incurred.

(n) **Nominee.** To hold securities and other property in bearer form or in the name of a Trustee or nominee with or without disclosure of any fiduciary relationship.

(o) **Miscellaneous Powers.** Generally, to do and perform any and all acts, things, or deeds which an individual could do with respect to property and which, in the judgment of the Trustee, may be necessary or proper for the investment, management, protection and promotion of the property of the trust estate.

(p) **Tax Elections.** Unless otherwise expressly directed hereunder, to exercise any tax option, allocation or election permitted by law as the Trustee determines in the Trustee's sole discretion.

(q) **Division and Distribution.** To make all allocations, distributions, or divisions contemplated by this instrument; to allocate, distribute and divide different kinds or disproportionate shares of property or undivided interests in property among the beneficiaries or trusts, in cash or in kind, or both, without regard to the income tax basis of specific property allocated to any beneficiary or trust, even though shares may as a result be composed differently, and to determine the value of any property so allocated, divided or distributed.

(r) **Reliance.** To rely upon any notice, certificate, affidavit, or other document or evidence believed by the Trustee to be genuine and accurate, in making any payment or distribution. The Trustee shall incur no liability for a disbursement or distribution made in good faith and without actual notice or knowledge of a changed condition or status affecting any person's interest in the trust or any other matter.

Court Supervision. The Trustee shall not be required to qualify before or be appointed by any court; nor shall the Trustee be required to obtain the order or approval of any court in the exercise of any power or discretion.

Periodic Accounting. The Trustee shall make reports at least annually to those beneficiaries who may receive current distributions, such reports to reflect the property held in trust, the receipts, disbursements, and distributions made during the accounting period, and such other information as may be necessary to convey the condition of and changes to the trust estate.

Beneficiary Under Disability. Where a beneficiary is under the disability of minority or, in the Trustee's opinion, any other legal, physical or mental disability, a parent, custodian or guardian who, entirely in the Trustee's discretion, is acceptable to the Trustee may, in carrying out the provisions of this Trust Agreement, act and receive notice in the beneficiary's place, and sign any instrument for the beneficiary.

Spendthrift Trusts. All trusts created under this Trust Agreement are spendthrift trusts. No beneficiary may anticipate, by assignment or otherwise, a beneficial interest in the principal or income of the trusts created hereunder; nor may any beneficiary sell, transfer, encumber, or in any way charge an interest in trust income or principal prior to actually receiving it. Neither the income nor the principal of any trust established hereunder shall be subject to any execution, garnishment, attachment, bankruptcy, claims for alimony or support, other legal proceeding of any character, legal sequestration, levy or sale, or in any other event or manner be applicable or subject, voluntarily or involuntarily, to the payment of a beneficiary's debts. The Trustee shall make distributions to or for each beneficiary according to the terms hereof, notwithstanding any purported sale, assignment, hypothecation, transfer, attachment, or judicial process.

Limitation on Distributions.

(a) **Support Obligation.** Any other provision of this Trust Agreement notwithstanding, no distribution shall be made which discharges, in whole or in part, the Trustee's legal obligations, from time to time existing, to support, educate or otherwise provide for any of the trust beneficiaries. When determining these legal obligations, the existence of the trust estate and funds made available by it shall not be taken into consideration.

(b) **Distribution to Trustee/Beneficiary.** Notwithstanding anything to the contrary in this Trust Agreement, no Trustee shall have the authority to make discretionary distributions to that person as beneficiary, except to the extent the distributions are for the beneficiary's health, maintenance, support or education. If the Trustee is otherwise in this Trust Agreement authorized to make a distribution beyond that standard, the distributions shall be so limited.

Rule Against Perpetuities.

Every trust created hereunder (or through the exercise of a power of appointment granted in this Trust Agreement) must vest not later than twenty-one (21) years after my death and descendants living at the time the trust created hereunder first becomes irrevocable. If a trust is not vested within that period, it will terminate as of the maximum vesting date. In the event of termination, the Trustee shall distribute each trust to its income beneficiaries determined at the time of distribution in the proportions to which they are entitled to receive income.

Out-of-State Properties.

If the Trustee must act in a jurisdiction in which a person or entity serving as Trustee is unable or unwilling to act, the other or others serving as Trustee may act in that jurisdiction. If no Trustee is able or willing to act, the Trustee may appoint an ancillary trustee for that jurisdiction and may confer upon the ancillary trustee such rights, powers, discretions and duties, exercisable without court order, to act with respect to such matters as the Trustee deems proper. The ancillary trustee shall be responsible to the Trustee for any property it administers. The Trustee may pay the ancillary trustee reasonable compensation for services and may absolve the ancillary trustee from any requirement to furnish bond or other security.

ARTICLE VIII

AMENDMENT AND REVOCATION OF TRUST

I may amend, revoke or modify this Trust Agreement in whole or in part by an instrument signed and acknowledged by me and delivered to the Trustee. Amendment or modification of the Trust Agreement shall be effective immediately upon delivery of the instrument to the Trustee, except that changes affecting the Trustee's duties, liabilities, or compensation shall not be effective without the Trustee's written consent. On my death, this Trust Agreement may no longer be amended or modified, and the trust created hereunder shall become irrevocable.

ARTICLE IX

MISCELLANEOUS PROVISIONS

Applicable Law. The validity, construction, and administration of each trust created hereunder shall be governed by the laws of the State of _____.

Adoption. For purposes of this Trust Agreement, a person shall be regarded as having been legally adopted by another only if the adoption is by court proceedings, the finality of which is not being contested by the adopting person.

Survival. Any person must survive by thirty (30) days for a gift made in this Trust Agreement which directly or indirectly requires such person's survival of another to be effective.

Education. "Education" shall include preparatory, collegiate, postgraduate, professional and vocational education; specialized formal or informal training in music, the stage, handicrafts, the arts or sports or athletic endeavors, whether by private instruction or otherwise; and any other activity, including foreign or domestic travel, which tends to develop the talents and potential of the beneficiary, regardless of age. Education shall also include all tuition, board, lodging fees, books and equipment, travel expenses and other expenses incidental thereto.

Executor. "Executor" shall include personal representative, executrix, administrator and administratrix.

Health. "Health" shall include medical, dental, hospital and nursing care expenses, and other expenses of invalidism, and distributions for the "health" of a beneficiary may, in the discretion of the Trustee include any part or all of the costs of purchasing or maintaining hospital or medical insurance and disability income insurance coverage for such beneficiary and/or any person in whom such beneficiary has an insurable interest.

Binding Agreement. This agreement shall extend to and be binding upon the heirs, executors, administrators, successors and assigns of the parties.

Use of Words. As used in this instrument, the masculine, feminine, and neuter gender, and the singular or plural of any word includes the others unless the context indicates otherwise.

Unenforceable Provision. If any provision of this Trust Agreement is unenforceable, the remaining provisions shall be given effect, unless to do so would produce an unreasonable result.

Titles, Headings, and Captions. All titles, headings, and captions used in this Trust Agreement have been included for convenience only and should not be construed in interpreting this instrument.

IN WITNESS WHEREOF, I as Grantor and Trustee have hereunto set my hand, on the day and year first above written in multiple originals.

_____ _____

Witness   Grantor

_____ _____

Witness   Trustee

STATE OF _____ §

§

COUNTY OF _____ §

BEFORE ME, the undersigned authority, on this day personally appeared _____, Grantor and Trustee, known to me to be the person whose name is subscribed to the foregoing instrument and acknowledged to me that he/she executed the same for the purposes and consideration therein expressed.

GIVEN UNDER MY HAND AND SEAL OF OFFICE this ____ day of _____, _____.

_____

Notary Public
My Commission Expires:

_____ LIVING TRUST

THIS AGREEMENT OF TRUST is entered into at _____, State of _____, this _____ day of _____, _____, by and between _____, as Grantor and Trustee. This Trust, as from time to time amended, shall be known as the "_____ LIVING TRUST dated _____, _____."

ARTICLE I

My Children. My Children are: _____

_____.

ARTICLE II

FUNDING

Initial Funding. I hereby transfer to Trustee the sum of Ten Dollars ($10.00).

Additional Funding. From time to time the trust may be funded with additional property by me or by any other person in any manner. All property transferred, assigned, conveyed or delivered to the Trustee shall be held, administered and distributed by the Trustee in accordance with the terms of this Trust Agreement.

ARTICLE III

ADMINISTRATION OF TRUST DURING MY LIFETIME

Distributions of Income. While I am living, the Trustee shall distribute the trust's net income as directed in writing by me from time to time. In default of such direction, the Trustee shall pay to or expend on behalf of me all of the trust's net income from the Trust quarterly or more frequently.

Distributions of Principal. The Trustee shall pay to or expend for my benefit such part or all of the principal of the trust as I may request, from time to time. In default of such direction, the Trustee shall pay to or expend for my benefit so much of the principal of the trust as the Trustee, determines to be necessary or advisable for my health, maintenance and support.

Use of Residential Property. If any real property used by me for residential purposes (whether on a full-time or part-time basis, including recreational property) becomes part of the trust estate, I shall have the right to use and occupy such property without rental or other accounting to the trust estate.

Distributions to My Children. The Trustee shall pay to or expend for the benefit of my minor Children so much of the principal of the trust as the Trustee, in his/her sole discretion, determines to be necessary for the education, health, maintenance and support of my Children. The Trustee shall make such discretionary distributions only after conferring with me. The trust distributions do not need to be equal.

ARTICLE IV

ADMINISTRATION OF TRUST UPON MY DEATH

Payment of Expenses, Claims and Taxes. Upon my death, the Trustee shall, upon the request of the Executor of my estate, pay such part or all of the expenses of the last illness, funeral, and burial, legally enforceable claims against me or my estate and estate administration expenses. The Trustee may also pay any estate, inheritance, or succession taxes, state, federal and foreign, or any other taxes together with interest and penalties thereon that are payable by reason of my death.

ARTICLE V

DISTRIBUTION OF TRUST TO MY CHILDREN

Tangible Personal Property. The Trustee shall distribute my tangible personal property in accordance with any written, signed and dated memorandum prepared by me. Any tangible personal property which is not disposed of by memorandum shall be distributed in equal shares to my surviving Children.

Specific Bequest. The Trustee shall distribute the following property to the named individuals:

_____ to _____

_____ to _____

If any of the individuals named does not survive me, the gift to that person will lapse and the property will pass as provided below.

Division of Trust Estate for My Children. The Trustee shall divide the remaining trust estate, including any additions to the Trust by reason of my death, into separate equal shares as follows: one share for each Child of mine who is then living, and one share for the then living descendants, collectively, of each deceased Child of mine with one or more descendants then living. The Trustee shall administer a share for each Child in a separate trust, and a share for the Descendants of each deceased Child, pursuant to the provisions of Article VI, following.

ARTICLE VI

TRUSTS FOR CHILDREN AND DESCENDANTS

Separate Trust for Child. Each trust for the benefit of a Child shall be administered and distributed upon the following terms:

(a) **Distributions to Child.** The Trustee shall distribute to the Child all of the trust's net income quarterly or more frequently and so much of the principal of the trust as the Trustee deems necessary to provide for the Child's health, maintenance, education and support.

When the Child attains age _____, the Trustee shall distribute to the Child _____ of the value of the then remaining trust estate.

When the Child attains age _____, the Trustee shall distribute to the Child the remaining trust estate.

(b) **Termination of Trust.** If not earlier terminated by distribution of the entire trust estate under the foregoing provisions, the trust shall terminate upon the death of the Child. The Trustee shall distribute the remaining trust estate to the Child's then living descendants, pursuant to the limitation described in subsection (c) hereof. If there are no descendants of the Child then living, the Trustee shall distribute the remaining trust estate to my then living descendants, per stirpes.

(c) **Distribution to Descendants of a Deceased Child.** Property which is to be distributed under this subsection to the descendants of a deceased Child shall be distributed, per stirpes, to those descendants living at the event causing the distribution hereunder.

Contingent Distribution. If my spouse, my Children and their descendants and all of my descendants are deceased, the trust estate then remaining shall be distributed, to the following individuals in the amounts specified:

_____ to_____

_____ to_____

ARTICLE VII

THE TRUSTEE

Successor Trustees. During my lifetime, if I cannot serve as Trustee, I will appoint a successor Trustee. If I do not appoint a successor trustee, or after my death, the successor trustee shall be _____. If

_____ is not able to serve, the successor trustee(s) shall be _____.
If the successor trustee fails or ceases to serve, _____
shall be successor trustee. If all successor trustees fail or cease to serve, a majority in number of the income beneficiaries of the trust at that time shall appoint a successor trustee. Any appointment under this section shall be by a signed, acknowledged instrument delivered to the successor trustee.

Removal of Trustee. During my life, I may remove a trustee at any time for any reason. After my death or if I am incapacitated and unable to remove the trustee, _____ _____ may remove the trustee. If _____ is not alive or is unable to exercise this power, _____ shall have the power to remove a trustee.

Resignation of Trustee. A Trustee may resign as to any one or more of the trusts created hereunder by giving written notice to all co-trustees then serving, if any, the current income beneficiaries, the successor trustee if identified in this Trust Agreement, and to those persons, if any, authorized in this Trust Agreement to appoint the successor trustee. Notice shall be delivered at least thirty (30) days prior to the date of resignation.

Trustee's Fees. The Trustee shall be entitled to reasonable fees commensurate with the Trustee's duties and responsibilities, taking into account the value and nature of the trust estate and the time and work involved. The Trustee shall be reimbursed for reasonable costs and expenses incurred in connection with fiduciary duties.

Bond. The Trustee shall not be required to furnish bond or other security.

Liability of Trustee. A Trustee shall only be liable for willful misconduct or gross negligence, and shall not be liable for breach of fiduciary duty by virtue of mistake or error in judgment.

Incapacity of Individual Trustee. This Section shall apply in the event a Trustee becomes unable to discharge the duties of Trustee by reason of accident, physical or mental illness or deterioration, or other cause, and does not resign. Upon certification by two medical doctors that each has examined the Trustee and has concluded that the Trustee is unable to discharge such duties, the Trustee shall cease to serve, as if the Trustee had resigned, effective the date of the certification.

ARTICLE VIII

TRUST ADMINISTRATION

Trustee Powers: Investment and Management of Trust Estate. Subject to any limitation stated elsewhere in this instrument, the Trustee shall have, with respect to each trust established hereunder, all of the powers granted to trustees by common law and by applicable statutes as amended from time to time. In addition, the trustee shall have the following powers:

(a) **Retain Property.** To retain any property received from any source, regardless of lack of diversification, risk, or nonproductivity.

(b) **Invest.** To invest the trust estate in any kind of property, without being limited by any law dealing with the character, risk, productivity, diversification, wasting nature of, or otherwise concerning, investments by trustees.

(c) **Sell.** By public offering or private negotiation, to sell, exchange, assign, transfer, or otherwise dispose of all or any real or personal trust property and give options for these purposes, for such price and on such terms, with such covenants of warranty and such security for deferred payment as the Trustee deems proper. To partition between the trust and any other owner, as the Trustee deems proper, any property in which the trust owns an undivided interest.

(d) **Lease.** To lease trust property for terms within or extending beyond the term of the trust, for any purpose.

(e) **Real Estate.** To operate, maintain, repair, rehabilitate, alter, erect, improve, or remove any improvements on real estate; to subdivide real estate; to grant easements, give consents, and enter into contracts relating to real estate or its use; and to release or dedicate any interest in real estate.

(f) **Borrow.** To borrow money for any purpose; to encumber or hypothecate trust property by mortgage, deed of trust, or otherwise; and to maintain, prepay, renew, or extend any indebtedness upon such terms as the Trustee deems appropriate.

(g) **Loans.** To lend money to any person or entity, including, but not limited to, a beneficiary hereunder, upon such terms and with such security as the Trustee deems advisable.

(h) **Securities.** To engage in all actions necessary to the effective administration of securities including, but not limited to, the authority to: vote securities in person or by proxy; engage in a voting trust or voting agreement; exercise any options, rights, or privileges pertaining to any trust property; and consent to or participate in mergers, consolidations, sales of assets, recapitalizations, reorganizations, dissolutions, or other alterations of corporate structure affecting securities held by the Trustee.

(i) **Business Powers.** To enter into, carry on, and expand or acquire additional interests in (through the investment or loan of trust funds) any business activity, in sole proprietorship, general or limited partnership, joint venture, corporate or other form (and to convert from one form to another), including, but not limited to, any business interest which may be contributed to the trust, to employ agents and confer upon them the authority to manage and operate such business activity without liability for the acts of any such agents or for any loss, liability or indebtedness of such business, if the agents are selected and retained with reasonable care; and to sell, liquidate, or otherwise terminate any business interest, including, but not limited to, the fulfillment of any agreement for the disposition of any such business interest.

(j) **Litigation.** To commence or defend at the expense of the trust such litigation with respect to the trust estate as the Trustee deems advisable.

(k) **Claims.** To collect, pay, contest, compromise, settle, renew, or abandon any claims or demands of or against the trust estate, on whatever terms the Trustee deems advisable.

(l) **Additional Property.** To receive from any source additional property which is acceptable to the Trustee, and add it to the trust estate.

(m) **Agents.** To employ attorneys, auditors, brokers, investment advisors, depositaries, and agents with or without discretionary powers, to employ a trust company or bank with trust powers as agent for the purpose of performing any delegable duties of the administration, and to pay all expenses and fees so incurred.

(n) **Nominee.** To hold securities and other property in bearer form or in the name of a Trustee or nominee with or without disclosure of any fiduciary relationship.

(o) **Miscellaneous Powers.** Generally, to do and perform any and all acts, things, or deeds which an individual could do with respect to property and which, in the judgment of the Trustee, may be necessary or proper for the investment, management, protection and promotion of the property of the trust estate.

(p) **Tax Elections.** Unless otherwise expressly directed hereunder, to exercise any tax option, allocation or election permitted by law as the Trustee determines in the Trustee's sole discretion.

(q) **Division and Distribution.** To make all allocations, distributions, or divisions contemplated by this instrument; to allocate, distribute and divide different kinds or disproportionate shares of property or undivided interests in property among the beneficiaries or trusts, in cash or in kind, or both, without regard to the income tax basis of specific property allocated to any beneficiary or trust, even though shares may as a result be composed differently, and to determine the value of any property so allocated, divided or distributed.

(r) **Reliance.** To rely upon any notice, certificate, affidavit, or other document or evidence believed by the Trustee to be genuine and accurate, in making any payment or distribution. The Trustee shall incur no liability for a disbursement or distribution made in good faith and without actual notice or knowledge of a changed condition or status affecting any person's interest in the trust or any other matter.

Court Supervision. The Trustee shall not be required to qualify before or be appointed by any court; nor shall the Trustee be required to obtain the order or approval of any court in the exercise of any power or discretion.

Periodic Accounting. The Trustee shall make reports at least annually to those beneficiaries who may receive current distributions, such reports to reflect the property held in trust, the receipts, disbursements, and distributions made during the accounting period, and such other information as may be necessary to convey the condition of and changes to the trust estate.

Beneficiary Under Disability. Where a beneficiary is under the disability of minority or, in the Trustee's opinion, any other legal, physical or mental disability, a parent, custodian or guardian who, entirely in the Trustee's discretion, is acceptable to the Trustee may, in carrying out the provisions of this Trust Agreement, act and receive notice in the beneficiary's place, and sign any instrument for the beneficiary.

Spendthrift Trusts. All trusts created under this Trust Agreement are spendthrift trusts. No beneficiary may anticipate, by assignment or otherwise, a beneficial interest in the principal or income of the trusts created hereunder; nor may any beneficiary sell, transfer, encumber, or in any way charge an interest in trust income or principal prior to actually receiving it. Neither the income nor the principal of any trust established hereunder shall be subject to any execution, garnishment, attachment, bankruptcy, claims for alimony or support, other legal proceeding of any character, legal sequestration, levy or sale, or in any other event or manner be applicable or subject, voluntarily or involuntarily, to the payment of a beneficiary's debts. The Trustee shall make distributions to or for each beneficiary according to the terms hereof, notwithstanding any purported sale, assignment, hypothecation, transfer, attachment, or judicial process.

Limitation on Distributions.

(a) **Support Obligation.** Any other provision of this Trust Agreement notwithstanding, no distribution shall be made which discharges, in whole or in part, the Trustee's legal obligations, from time to time existing, to support, educate or otherwise provide for any of the trust beneficiaries. When determining these legal obligations, the existence of the trust estate and funds made available by it shall not be taken into consideration.

(b) **Distribution to Trustee/Beneficiary.** Notwithstanding anything to the contrary in this Trust Agreement, no Trustee shall have the authority to make discretionary distributions to that person as beneficiary, except to the extent the distributions are for the beneficiary's health, maintenance, support or education. If the Trustee is otherwise in this Trust Agreement authorized to make a distribution beyond that standard, the distributions shall be so limited.

Rule Against Perpetuities. Every trust created hereunder (or through the exercise of a power of appointment granted in this Trust Agreement) must vest not later than twenty-one (21) years after my death and descendants living at the time the trust created hereunder first becomes irrevocable. If a trust is not vested within that period, it will terminate as of the maximum vesting date. In the event of termination, the Trustee shall distribute each trust to its income beneficiaries determined at the time of distribution in the proportions to which they are entitled to receive income.

Out-of-State Properties. If the Trustee must act in a jurisdiction in which a person or entity serving as Trustee is unable or unwilling to act, the other or others serving as Trustee may act in that jurisdiction. If no Trustee is able or willing to act, the Trustee may appoint an ancillary trustee for that jurisdiction and may confer upon the ancillary trustee such rights, powers, discretions and duties, exercisable without court order, to act with respect to such matters as the Trustee deems proper. The ancillary trustee shall be responsible to the Trustee for any property it administers. The Trustee may pay the ancillary trustee reasonable compensation for services and may absolve the ancillary trustee from any requirement to furnish bond or other security.

ARTICLE IX

AMENDMENT AND REVOCATION OF TRUST

I may amend, revoke or modify this Trust Agreement in whole or in part by an instrument signed and acknowledged by me and delivered to the Trustee. Amendment or modification of the Trust Agreement shall be effective immediately upon delivery of the instrument to the Trustee, except that changes affecting the Trustee's duties, liabilities, or compensation shall not be effective without the Trustee's written consent. On my death, this Trust Agreement may no longer be amended or modified, and the trust created hereunder shall become irrevocable.

ARTICLE X

MISCELLANEOUS PROVISIONS

Applicable Law. The validity, construction, and administration of each trust created hereunder shall be governed by the laws of the State of _____.

Adoption. For purposes of this Trust Agreement, a person shall be regarded as having been legally adopted by another only if the adoption is by court proceedings, the finality of which is not being contested by the adopting person.

Survival. Any person must survive by thirty (30) days for a gift made in this Trust Agreement which directly or indirectly requires such person's survival of another to

be effective.

Education. "Education" shall include preparatory, collegiate, postgraduate, professional and vocational education; specialized formal or informal training in music, the stage, handicrafts, the arts or sports or athletic endeavors, whether by private instruction or otherwise; and any other activity, including foreign or domestic travel, which tends to develop the talents and potential of the beneficiary, regardless of age. Education shall also include all tuition, board, lodging fees, books and equipment, travel expenses and other expenses incidental thereto.

Executor. "Executor" shall include personal representative, executrix, administrator and administratrix.

Health. "Health" shall include medical, dental, hospital, and nursing care expenses, and other expenses of invalidism, and distributions for the "health" of a beneficiary may, in the discretion of the Trustee include any part or all of the costs of purchasing or maintaining hospital or medical insurance and disability income insurance coverage for such beneficiary and/or any person in whom such beneficiary has an insurable interest.

Binding Agreement. This agreement shall extend to and be binding upon the heirs, executors, administrators, successors and assigns of the parties.

Use of Words. As used in this instrument, the masculine, feminine, and neuter gender, and the singular or plural of any word includes the others unless the context indicates otherwise.

Unenforceable Provision. If any provision of this Trust Agreement is unenforceable, the remaining provisions shall be given effect, unless to do so would produce an unreasonable result.

Titles, Headings, and Captions. All titles, headings, and captions used in this Trust Agreement have been included for convenience only and should not be construed in interpreting this instrument.

IN WITNESS WHEREOF, I as Grantor and Trustee have hereunto set my hand, on the day and year first above written in multiple originals.

_____   _____

Witness   Grantor

_____   _____

Witness   Trustee

STATE OF _____ §

                                                         §

COUNTY OF _____ §

BEFORE ME, the undersigned authority, on this day personally appeared _____, Grantor and Trustee, known to me to be the person whose name is subscribed to the foregoing instrument and acknowledged to me that he/she executed the same for the purposes and consideration therein expressed.

GIVEN UNDER MY HAND AND SEAL OF OFFICE this ____ day of _____, _____.

_____

Notary Public
My Commission Expires:

MEMORANDUM OF DISPOSITION
OF TANGIBLE PERSONAL PROPERTY

Pursuant to the terms of my Living Trust dated _____ , _____ , I have requested the distribution of certain items of my tangible property in accordance with a writing or memorandum, and this memorandum is made for such purpose. If the named beneficiary of a particular item does not survive me by more than thirty days, such item shall be disposed of as though it had not been listed herein.

Description Of Item of Tangible Personal Property	Name of Beneficiary and Address

Dated:_____

_____   _____
Witness   Signature of property owner

_____
Witness

_____
Witness

INSTRUCTIONS FOR USE OF PERSONAL PROPERTY MEMORANDUM

1. For such a memorandum to be effective, your trust must expressly refer to disposition of your personal property by a memorandum or written list.

2. The memorandum should not include items already specifically disposed of by you in your Will or Trust.

3. This memorandum is designed for disposing of such items as jewelry, furniture, antiques, artwork, china, silverware, sports equipment, coin and stamp collections, and similar items of household goods and personal effects. This memorandum is not intended to apply to the disposition of money, of promissory notes or other evidence of indebtedness, of real estate, of securities, or of any property used in a trade or business.

4. The memorandum should be dated and signed by you.

5. You should clearly describe each item so that it can be easily identified and will not be confused with another similar item.

6. Each designated beneficiary should be identified by his or her proper name and relationship to you. The address of the beneficiary should be added if he or she does not live in the same household as you.

7. You should consider providing for an alternative beneficiary if the first designated beneficiary does not survive you.

8. You may change the recipients or property designated in the memorandum from time to time or revise or revoke the entire memorandum. Changes should be made only by a new memorandum patterned after this form and the old memorandum should be destroyed. Changes should never be made by striking through an item or by other alterations made on the memorandum after it has been executed; this might create a question as to the validity of the entire memorandum since it might not be possible at a later time to determine whether you or someone else made such changes.

9. If it is desired that a named beneficiary should receive the property only if he or she survives both you and some other person (such as your spouse), that desire should be expressed after the beneficiary's name.

AMENDMENT
TO
THE _____ LIVING TRUST

Dated _____, _____

This Amendment to THE _____ LIVING TRUST, dated _____, _____ (the "Trust"), by _____ _____, as Grantor and as Trustee. Pursuant to the power of amendment reserved by me in Article _____ of the Trust, Grantor hereby amends the Trust as follows:

ITEM 1.

Grantor hereby deletes the following paragraph of the Trust in its entirety, and substitutes in its place the following:

Deleted paragraph:

Replacement paragraph:

ITEM 2.

Grantor hereby adds the following paragraph to the Trust:

IN WITNESS WHEREOF, _____ has hereunder caused his/her name to be subscribed as Grantor and as Trustee of this Amendment to THE _____ LIVING TRUST, dated _____, _____, at the City of _____, County of _____, State of _____, on this _____ day of _____, _____.

_____   _____
Witness   Grantor

_____   _____
Witness   Trustee

THE STATE OF _____   §
                                         §
COUNTY OF _____   §

BEFORE ME, the undersigned authority, a Notary Public in and for said County and State, on this day personally appeared _____, known to me to be the person whose name is subscribed to the annexed or foregoing instrument, and acknowledged to me that he/she executed the same for the purposes and consideration therein expressed and in the capacities therein stated.

GIVEN UNDER MY HAND AND SEAL OF OFFICE, this the _____ day of _____, _____.

_____
Notary Public
My commission expires:

REVOCATION OF

THE _____LIVING TRUST

On _____, _____, I, _____,
as trustee and grantor, executed a certain trust agreement, wherein I reserved the right at any time
or times to amend or revoke the trust agreement in whole or in part by an instrument in writing
delivered to the trustee.

Pursuant to the right reserved to me under the trust agreement, I hereby revoke the trust
agreement in its entirety and direct that the trust property held thereunder be conveyed by the
trustee to me.

IN WITNESS WHEREOF, I have signed this revocation this _____ day of
_____, _____.

_____   _____
Witness   Grantor

_____
Witness

STATE OF _____ §
                                 §
COUNTY OF ___ _____ §

I, _____, Notary Public, hereby certify that
_____, personally known to me to be the same per-
son whose name is signed to the foregoing instrument, appeared before me this day in person and
acknowledged that he/she signed the instrument as his/her free and voluntary act, for the uses
and purposes therein set forth.

Given under my hand and official seal this _____ day of _____, _____.

_____
Notary Public
My commission expires:

ASSIGNMENT OF PERSONAL PROPERTY

      The undersigned does hereby transfer and assign, without consideration and solely in order to change formal title, all of his/her right, title and interest in and to the following property to _____, Trustee of the _____LIVING TRUST, dated _____, _____, and any amendments thereto:

      All personal property now or hereafter located in the principal and any other residences of the undersigned.

Dated this _____ day of _____, _____.

_____
(Name)

STATE OF _____ §
                                             §
COUNTY OF _____ §

      Subscribed and acknowledged before me this _____ day of _____, _____, by _____ , known to me to be ther person whose name is subscribed to the foregoing instrument and acknowledged to me that he/she executed the same for the purposes and consideration therein expressed.

      GIVEN UNDER MY HAND AND SEAL OF OFFICE this _____ day of _____, _____.

_____
Notary Public
My Commission Expires:

Personal Property Assignment

Date: _____

    The undersigned, _____,
as assignor(s), in consideration of the sum of one dollar, receipt of which is acknowledged, and
other good and valuable consideration, hereby assigns, transfers, and delivers to _____
_____ as assignee, the following goods:

Assignor(s):   Assignee:

_____   _____

_____

_____

Personal Property Assignment

Date: _____

    The undersigned, _____,
as assignor, in consideration of the sum of one dollar, receipt of which is acknowledged, and other good and valuable consideration, hereby assigns, transfers, and delivers to _____
_____ as assignees, the following goods:

_____ shall

own the above-listed goods:

    ❑   as husband and wife, in an estate by the entireties.

    ❑   as joint tenants with full rights of survivorship.

    ❑   as husband and wife, as joint tenants with full rights of survivorship.

Assignor: Assignees:

_____   _____

                                          _____

                                          _____

APPENDIX B
LIVING TRUST TAX FORMS

The following pages contain tax forms that relate to living trusts:

Explanation of State Death Taxes Including
State Death Tax Credit Table

STATE DEATH TAXES

Each state imposes some form of death tax on a decedent's estate. There are three types of state death taxes: the pick-up tax, the estate tax and the inheritance tax.

The Pick-Up Tax

The federal government permits a limited credit against federal estate taxes for death taxes paid to the states. The amount of this state tax credit is calculated through a formula established by the federal government. A chart illustrating how this credit is calculated follows. Several states have a death tax that is equal to the maximum state tax credit that the federal government permits. This is referred to as a "pick-up" tax. The following states have pick-up taxes:

Alabama	Florida	Missouri	Texas
Alaska	Georgia	Nevada	Utah
Arizona	Hawaii	New Mexico	Vermont
Arkansas	Idaho	North Dakota	Virginia
California	Illinois	Oregon	Washington
Colorado	Maine	Rhode Island	West Virginia
District of	Minnesota	South Carolina	Wisconsin
Columbia			Wyoming

State Estate Tax

The states listed below impose an estate tax on their residents. The estate tax is calculated in the same manner as the federal estate tax. It is a tax on the value of the assets owned by the decedent at the date of his death. Often the estate tax imposed by a state is much more than the state death tax credit that the federal government allows. Estate tax states are:

Massachusetts	Ohio
Mississippi	Oklahoma
New York	

State Inheritance Tax

Several states impose an inheritance tax. This type of tax is levied directly on the beneficiaries who receive the assets. Often the amount of the inheritance tax depends upon the relationship of the beneficiary to the decedent. Spouses, children, grandchildren and parents are often taxed at a lower rate than sisters, brothers, nieces, nephews and nonrelatives. The following states use the inheritance tax system:

Connecticut	Louisiana	New Jersey
Delaware	Maryland	North Carolina
Indiana	Michigan	Pennsylvania
Iowa	Montana	South Dakota
Kansas	Nebraska	Tennessee
Kentucky	New Hampshire	

No matter which type of tax that a state imposes, you need to be aware of the tax and the potential impact of that tax on your estate. You can obtain specific information on your state's form of tax and the rate of tax by contacting the state treasurer or comptroller or the state tax department.

STATE DEATH TAX CREDIT

Adjustable Taxable Estate [1]		Credit =	+ %	Of Excess Over
At Least	But Less Than			
$ 0	$ 40,000	$ 0	0	$ 0
40,000	90,000	0	.8	40,000
90,000	140,000	400	1.6	90,000
140,000	240,000	1,200	2.4	140,000
240,000	440,000	3,600	3.2	240,000
440,000	640,000	10,000	4.0	440,000
640,000	840,000	18,000	4.8	640,000
840,000	1,040,000	27,600	5.6	840,000
1,040,000	1,540,000	38,800	6.4	1,040,000
1,540,000	2,040,000	70,800	7.2	1,540,000
2,040,000	2,540,000	106,800	8.0	2,040,000
2,540,000	3,040,000	146,800	8.8	2,540,000
3,040,000	3,540,000	190,800	9.6	3,040,000
3,540,000	4,040,000	238,800	10.4	3,540,000
4,040,000	5,040,000	290,800	11.2	4,040,000
5,040,000	6,040,000	402,800	12.0	5,040,000
6,040,000	7,040,000	522,800	12.8	6,040,000
7,040,000	8,040,000	650,800	13.6	7,040,000
8,040,000	9,040,000	786,800	14.4	8,040,000
9,040,000	10,040,000	930,800	15.2	9,040,000
10,040,000	* * * * *	1,082,800	16.0	10,040,000

[1] The adjusted taxable estate is the taxable estate reduced by $60,000.

Explanation of Federal Estate Taxes Including
Federal Estate and Gift Tax Schedule

FEDERAL ESTATE TAX

As discussed throughout the text, all property owned by you at your death, probate and non-probate, is subject to the federal estate tax at your death. The federal estate tax applies to all estates. However, the law grants you a unified credit and your estate does not have to pay tax on an amount up to that credit. Until 1998, the amount of the unified credits has been $600,000. However, the Taxpayer Relief act of 1997 raises the amount of the unified credit in increments until 2006 when it will reach $1,000,000. The following is a chart of the amount of the unified credit for each year until 2006.

Year of death or gift	Amount
1998	$625,000
1999	$650,000
2000-2001	$675,000
2002-2003	$700,000
2004	$850,000
2005	$950,000
2006	$1,000,000

The estate tax is not an income tax. It is a tax on all of the assets that you have accumulated during your lifetime and that you own when you die. The estate tax is a tax on your assets but must be paid in cash to the IRS nine months after you die.

The following schedule shows how the estate tax is calculated and how it applies to estates of various sizes. You can see that after the unified credit amount has been reached, the next dollar is taxed at thirty-seven percent.

If your estate is worth more than the amount of the unified credit you should consult an experienced estate tax professional. The cost of obtaining such advice is greatly outweighed by the estate taxes that good planning can help to avoid.

FEDERAL ESTATE AND GIFT TAX SCHEDULE

Column A	Column B	Column C	Column D
Taxable amount over	Taxable amount not over	Tax on amount in Column A	Rate of tax on excess over amount in Column A Percent
$ 0	$ 10,000	$ 0	18
10,000	20,000	1,800	20
20,000	40,000	3,800	22
40,000	60,000	8,200	24
60,000	80,000	13,000	26
80,000	100,000	18,200	28
100,000	150,000	23,800	30
150,000	250,000	38,800	32
250,000	500,000	70,800	34
500,000	750,000	155,800	37
750,000	1,000,000	248,300	39
1,000,000	1,250,000	345,800	41
1,250,000	1,500,000	448,800	43
1,500,000	2,000,000	555,800	45
2,000,000	2,500,000	780,800	49
2,500,000	3,000,000	1,025,800	53
3,000,000	* * * * *	1,290,800	55

Total tax is equal to the amount in Column C
plus amount in Column D

Form **SS-4**

(Rev. December 1995)

Department of the Treasury
Internal Revenue Service

Application for Employer Identification Number

(For use by employers, corporations, partnerships, trusts, estates, churches, government agencies, certain individuals, and others. See instructions.)

▶ **Keep a copy for your records.**

EIN

OMB No. 1545-0003

Please type or print clearly.

1 Name of applicant (Legal name) (See instructions.)

2 Trade name of business (if different from name on line 1)

3 Executor, trustee, "care of" name

4a Mailing address (street address) (room, apt., or suite no.)

5a Business address (if different from address on lines 4a and 4b)

4b City, state, and ZIP code

5b City, state, and ZIP code

6 County and state where principal business is located

7 Name of principal officer, general partner, grantor, owner, or trustor—SSN required (See instructions.) ▶

8a Type of entity (Check only one box.) (See instructions.)
☐ Sole proprietor (SSN) _____
☐ Partnership   ☐ Personal service corp.
☐ REMIC   ☐ Limited liability co.
☐ State/local government   ☐ National Guard
☐ Other nonprofit organization (specify) ▶ _____ (enter GEN if applicable) _____
☐ Other (specify) ▶

☐ Estate (SSN of decedent) _____
☐ Plan administrator-SSN _____
☐ Other corporation (specify) ▶ _____
☐ Trust   ☐ Farmers' cooperative
☐ Federal Government/military ☐ Church or church-controlled organization

8b If a corporation, name the state or foreign country (if applicable) where incorporated

State

Foreign country

9 Reason for applying (Check only one box.)
☐ Started new business (specify) ▶ _____
_____
☐ Hired employees
☐ Created a pension plan (specify type) ▶

☐ Banking purpose (specify) ▶ _____
☐ Changed type of organization (specify) ▶ _____
☐ Purchased going business
☐ Created a trust (specify) ▶ _____
☐ Other (specify) ▶

10 Date business started or acquired (Mo., day, year) (See instructions.)

11 Closing month of accounting year (See instructions.)

12 First date wages or annuities were paid or will be paid (Mo., day, year). **Note:** *If applicant is a withholding agent, enter date income will first be paid to nonresident alien. (Mo., day, year)* . . . . ▶

13 Highest number of employees expected in the next 12 months. **Note:** *If the applicant does not expect to have any employees during the period, enter -0-. (See instructions.)* . . . ▶

Nonagricultural	Agricultural	Household

14 Principal activity (See instructions.) ▶

15 Is the principal business activity manufacturing? . . . . ☐ Yes ☐ No
If "Yes," principal product and raw material used ▶

16 To whom are most of the products or services sold? Please check the appropriate box.   ☐ Business (wholesale)
☐ Public (retail)   ☐ Other (specify) ▶   ☐ N/A

17a Has the applicant ever applied for an identification number for this or any other business? . . . . ☐ Yes ☐ No
Note: *If "Yes," please complete lines 17b and 17c.*

17b If you checked "Yes" on line 17a, give applicant's legal name and trade name shown on prior application, if different from line 1 or 2 above.
Legal name ▶   Trade name ▶

17c Approximate date when and city and state where the application was filed. Enter previous employer identification number if known.
Approximate date when filed (Mo., day, year) | City and state where filed | Previous EIN

Under penalties of perjury, I declare that I have examined this application, and to the best of my knowledge and belief, it is true, correct, and complete.

Business telephone number (include area code)

Fax telephone number (include area code)

Name and title (Please type or print clearly.) ▶

Signature ▶   Date ▶

Note: *Do not write below this line. For official use only.*

Please leave blank ▶	Geo.	Ind.	Class	Size	Reason for applying

For Paperwork Reduction Act Notice, see page 4.   Cat. No. 16055N   Form **SS-4** (Rev. 12-95)

139

General Instructions

Section references are to the Internal Revenue Code unless otherwise noted.

Purpose of Form

Use Form SS-4 to apply for an employer identification number (EIN). An EIN is a nine-digit number (for example, 12-3456789) assigned to sole proprietors, corporations, partnerships, estates, trusts, and other entities for filing and reporting purposes. The information you provide on this form will establish your filing and reporting requirements.

Who Must File

You must file this form if you have not obtained an EIN before and:

● You pay wages to one or more employees including household employees.

● You are required to have an EIN to use on any return, statement, or other document, even if you are not an employer.

● You are a withholding agent required to withhold taxes on income, other than wages, paid to a nonresident alien (individual, corporation, partnership, etc.). A withholding agent may be an agent, broker, fiduciary, manager, tenant, or spouse, and is required to file **Form 1042,** Annual Withholding Tax Return for U.S. Source Income of Foreign Persons.

● You file **Schedule C,** Profit or Loss From Business, or **Schedule F,** Profit or Loss From Farming, of **Form 1040,** U.S. Individual Income Tax Return, **and** have a Keogh plan or are required to file excise, employment, information, or alcohol, tobacco, or firearms returns.

The following must use EINs even if they do not have any employees:

● State and local agencies who serve as tax reporting agents for public assistance recipients, under Rev. Proc. 80-4, 1980-1 C.B. 581, should obtain a separate EIN for this reporting. See **Household employer** on page 3.

● Trusts, except the following:

1. Certain grantor-owned revocable trusts. (See the **Instructions for Form 1041.**)

2. Individual Retirement Arrangement (IRA) trusts, unless the trust has to file **Form 990-T,** Exempt Organization Business Income Tax Return. (See the **Instructions for Form 990-T.**)

3. Certain trusts that are considered household employers can use the trust EIN to report and pay the social security and Medicare taxes, Federal unemployment tax (FUTA) and withheld Federal income tax. A separate EIN is not necessary.

● Estates

● Partnerships

● REMICs (real estate mortgage investment conduits) (See the **Instructions for Form 1066,** U.S. Real Estate Mortgage Investment Conduit Income Tax Return.)

● Corporations

● Nonprofit organizations (churches, clubs, etc.)

● Farmers' cooperatives

● Plan administrators (A plan administrator is the person or group of persons specified as the administrator by the instrument under which the plan is operated.)

When To Apply for a New EIN

New Business.—If you become the new owner of an existing business, **do not** use the EIN of the former owner. IF YOU ALREADY HAVE AN EIN, USE THAT NUMBER. If you do not have an EIN, apply for one on this form. If you become the "owner" of a corporation by acquiring its stock, use the corporation's EIN.

Changes in Organization or Ownership.—If you already have an EIN, you may need to get a new one if either the organization or ownership of your business changes. If you incorporate a sole proprietorship or form a partnership, you must get a new EIN. However, **do not** apply for a new EIN if you change only the name of your business.

Note: *If you are electing to be an "S corporation," be sure you file **Form 2553,** Election by a Small Business Corporation.*

File Only One Form SS-4.—File only one Form SS-4, regardless of the number of businesses operated or trade names under which a business operates. However, each corporation in an affiliated group must file a separate application.

EIN Applied For, But Not Received.—If you do not have an EIN by the time a return is due, write "Applied for" and the date you applied in the space shown for the number. **Do not** show your social security number as an EIN on returns.

If you do not have an EIN by the time a tax deposit is due, send your payment to the Internal Revenue Service Center for your filing area. (See **Where To Apply** below.) Make your check or money order payable to Internal Revenue Service and show your name (as shown on Form SS-4), address, type of tax, period covered, and date you applied for an EIN. Send an explanation with the deposit.

For more information about EINs, see **Pub. 583,** Starting a Business and Keeping Records, and **Pub. 1635,** Understanding Your EIN.

How To Apply

You can apply for an EIN either by mail or by telephone. You can get an EIN immediately by calling the Tele-TIN phone number for the service center for your state, or you can send the completed Form SS-4 directly to the service center to receive your EIN in the mail.

Application by Tele-TIN.—Under the Tele-TIN program, you can receive your EIN over the telephone and use it immediately to file a return or make a payment. To receive an EIN by phone, complete Form SS-4, then call the Tele-TIN phone number listed for your state under **Where To Apply.** The person making the call must be authorized to sign the form. (See **Signature block** on page 4.)

An IRS representative will use the information from the Form SS-4 to establish your account and assign you an EIN. Write the number you are given on the upper right-hand corner of the form, sign and date it.

*Mail or FAX the signed SS-4 **within 24 hours** to the Tele-TIN Unit at the service center address for your state. The IRS representative will give you the FAX number. The FAX numbers are also listed in Pub. 1635.*

Taxpayer representatives can receive their client's EIN by phone if they first send a facsimile (FAX) of a completed **Form 2848,** Power of Attorney and Declaration of Representative, or **Form 8821,** Tax Information Authorization, to the Tele-TIN unit. The Form 2848 or Form 8821 will be used solely to release the EIN to the representative authorized on the form.

Application by Mail.—Complete Form SS-4 at least 4 to 5 weeks before you will need an EIN. Sign and date the application and mail it to the service center address for your state. You will receive your EIN in the mail in approximately 4 weeks.

Where To Apply

The Tele-TIN phone numbers listed below will involve a long-distance charge to callers outside of the local calling area and can be used only to apply for an EIN. THE NUMBERS MAY CHANGE WITHOUT NOTICE. Use 1-800-829-1040 to verify a number or to ask about an application by mail or other Federal tax matters.

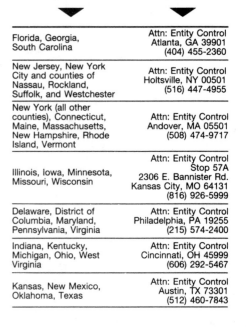

If your principal business, office or agency, or legal residence in the case of an individual, is located in: ▼	Call the Tele-TIN phone number shown or file with the Internal Revenue Service Center at: ▼
Florida, Georgia, South Carolina	Attn: Entity Control Atlanta, GA 39901 (404) 455-2360
New Jersey, New York City and counties of Nassau, Rockland, Suffolk, and Westchester	Attn: Entity Control Holtsville, NY 00501 (516) 447-4955
New York (all other counties), Connecticut, Maine, Massachusetts, New Hampshire, Rhode Island, Vermont	Attn: Entity Control Andover, MA 05501 (508) 474-9717
Illinois, Iowa, Minnesota, Missouri, Wisconsin	Attn: Entity Control Stop 57A 2306 E. Bannister Rd. Kansas City, MO 64131 (816) 926-5999
Delaware, District of Columbia, Maryland, Pennsylvania, Virginia	Attn: Entity Control Philadelphia, PA 19255 (215) 574-2400
Indiana, Kentucky, Michigan, Ohio, West Virginia	Attn: Entity Control Cincinnati, OH 45999 (606) 292-5467
Kansas, New Mexico, Oklahoma, Texas	Attn: Entity Control Austin, TX 73301 (512) 460-7843

	Attn: Entity Control
Alaska, Arizona, California (counties of Alpine, Amador, Butte, Calaveras, Colusa, Contra Costa, Del Norte, El Dorado, Glenn, Humboldt, Lake, Lassen, Marin, Mendocino, Modoc, Napa, Nevada, Placer, Plumas, Sacramento, San Joaquin, Shasta, Sierra, Siskiyou, Solano, Sonoma, Sutter, Tehama, Trinity, Yolo, and Yuba), Colorado, Idaho, Montana, Nebraska, Nevada, North Dakota, Oregon, South Dakota, Utah, Washington, Wyoming	Attn: Entity Control Mail Stop 6271-T P.O. Box 9950 Ogden, UT 84409 (801) 620-7645
California (all other counties), Hawaii	Attn: Entity Control Fresno, CA 93888 (209) 452-4010
Alabama, Arkansas, Louisiana, Mississippi, North Carolina, Tennessee	Attn: Entity Control Memphis, TN 37501 (901) 365-5970

If you have no legal residence, principal place of business, or principal office or agency in any state, file your form with the Internal Revenue Service Center, Philadelphia, PA 19255 or call 215-574-2400.

Specific Instructions

The instructions that follow are for those items that are not self-explanatory. Enter N/A (nonapplicable) on the lines that do not apply.

Line 1.—Enter the legal name of the entity applying for the EIN exactly as it appears on the social security card, charter, or other applicable legal document.

Individuals.—Enter the first name, middle initial, and last name. If you are a sole proprietor, enter your individual name, not your business name. Do not use abbreviations or nicknames.

Trusts.—Enter the name of the trust.

Estate of a decedent.—Enter the name of the estate.

Partnerships.—Enter the legal name of the partnership as it appears in the partnership agreement. **Do not** list the names of the partners on line 1. See the specific instructions for line 7.

Corporations.—Enter the corporate name as it appears in the corporation charter or other legal document creating it.

Plan administrators.—Enter the name of the plan administrator. A plan administrator who already has an EIN should use that number.

Line 2.—Enter the trade name of the business if different from the legal name. The trade name is the "doing business as" name.

Note: *Use the full legal name on line 1 on all tax returns filed for the entity. However, if you enter a trade name on line 2 and choose to use the trade name instead of the legal name, enter the trade name on all returns you file. To prevent processing delays and errors, **always** use either the legal name only or the trade name only on all tax returns.*

Line 3.—Trusts enter the name of the trustee. Estates enter the name of the executor, administrator, or other fiduciary. If the entity applying has a designated person to receive tax information, enter that person's name as the "care of"

person. Print or type the first name, middle initial, and last name.

Line 7.—Enter the first name, middle initial, last name, and social security number (SSN) of a principal officer if the business is a corporation; of a general partner if a partnership; or of a grantor, owner, or trustor if a trust.

Line 8a.—Check the box that best describes the type of entity applying for the EIN. If not specifically mentioned, check the "Other" box and enter the type of entity. Do not enter N/A.

Sole proprietor.—Check this box if you file Schedule C or F (Form 1040) and have a Keogh plan, or are required to file excise, employment, information, or alcohol, tobacco, or firearms returns. Enter your SSN in the space provided.

REMIC.—Check this box if the entity has elected to be treated as a real estate mortgage investment conduit (REMIC). See the **Instructions for Form 1066** for more information.

Other nonprofit organization.—Check this box if the nonprofit organization is other than a church or church-controlled organization and specify the type of nonprofit organization (for example, an educational organization).

If the organization also seeks tax-exempt status, you must file either **Package 1023** or **Package 1024,** Application for Recognition of Exemption. Get **Pub. 557,** Tax-Exempt Status for Your Organization, for more information.

Group exemption number (GEN).—If the organization is covered by a group exemption letter, enter the four-digit GEN. (Do not confuse the GEN with the nine-digit EIN.) If you do not know the GEN, contact the parent organization. Get Pub. 557 for more information about group exemption numbers.

Withholding agent.—If you are a withholding agent required to file Form 1042, check the "Other" box and enter "Withholding agent."

Personal service corporation.—Check this box if the entity is a personal service corporation. An entity is a personal service corporation for a tax year only if:

● The principal activity of the entity during the testing period (prior tax year) for the tax year is the performance of personal services substantially by employee-owners, and

● The employee-owners own 10% of the fair market value of the outstanding stock in the entity on the last day of the testing period.

Personal services include performance of services in such fields as health, law, accounting, or consulting. For more information about personal service corporations, see the **Instructions for Form 1120,** U.S. Corporation Income Tax Return, and **Pub. 542,** Tax Information on Corporations.

Limited liability co.—See the definition of limited liability company in the **Instructions for Form 1065.** If you are classified as a partnership for Federal income tax

purposes, mark the "Limited liability co." checkbox. If you are classified as a corporation for Federal income tax purposes, mark the "Other corporation" checkbox and write "Limited liability co." in the space provided.

Plan administrator.—If the plan administrator is an individual, enter the plan administrator's SSN in the space provided.

Other corporation.—This box is for any corporation other than a personal service corporation. If you check this box, enter the type of corporation (such as insurance company) in the space provided.

Household employer.—If you are an individual, check the "Other" box and enter "Household employer" and your SSN. If you are a state or local agency serving as a tax reporting agent for public assistance recipients who become household employers, check the "Other" box and enter "Household employer agent." If you are a trust that qualifies as a household employer, you do not need a separate EIN for reporting tax information relating to household employees; use the EIN of the trust.

Line 9.—Check only **one** box. Do not enter N/A.

Started new business.—Check this box if you are starting a new business that requires an EIN. If you check this box, enter the type of business being started. **Do not** apply if you already have an EIN and are only adding another place of business.

Hired employees.—Check this box if the existing business is requesting an EIN because it has hired or is hiring employees and is therefore required to file employment tax returns. **Do not** apply if you already have an EIN and are only hiring employees. For information on the applicable employment taxes for family members, see **Circular E,** Employer's Tax Guide (Publication 15).

Created a pension plan.—Check this box if you have created a pension plan and need this number for reporting purposes. Also, enter the type of plan created.

Banking purpose.—Check this box if you are requesting an EIN for banking purposes only, and enter the banking purpose (for example, a bowling league for depositing dues or an investment club for dividend and interest reporting).

Changed type of organization.—Check this box if the business is changing its type of organization, for example, if the business was a sole proprietorship and has been incorporated or has become a partnership. If you check this box, specify in the space provided the type of change made, for example, "from sole proprietorship to partnership."

Purchased going business.—Check this box if you purchased an existing business. **Do not** use the former owner's EIN. **Do not** apply for a new EIN if you already have one. Use your own EIN.

Created a trust.—Check this box if you created a trust, and enter the type of trust created.

141

Note: *Do not file this form if you are the grantor/owner of certain revocable trusts. You must use your SSN for the trust. See the Instructions for Form 1041.*

Other (specify).—Check this box if you are requesting an EIN for any reason other than those for which there are checkboxes, and enter the reason.

Line 10.—If you are starting a new business, enter the starting date of the business. If the business you acquired is already operating, enter the date you acquired the business. Trusts should enter the date the trust was legally created. Estates should enter the date of death of the decedent whose name appears on line 1 or the date when the estate was legally funded.

Line 11.—Enter the last month of your accounting year or tax year. An accounting or tax year is usually 12 consecutive months, either a calendar year or a fiscal year (including a period of 52 or 53 weeks). A calendar year is 12 consecutive months ending on December 31. A fiscal year is either 12 consecutive months ending on the last day of any month other than December or a 52-53 week year. For more information on accounting periods, see **Pub. 538,** Accounting Periods and Methods.

Individuals.—Your tax year generally will be a calendar year.

Partnerships.—Partnerships generally must adopt the tax year of either (a) the majority partners; (b) the principal partners; (c) the tax year that results in the least aggregate (total) deferral of income; or (d) some other tax year. (See the **Instructions for Form 1065,** U.S. Partnership Return of Income, for more information.)

REMIC.—REMICs must have a calendar year as their tax year.

Personal service corporations.—A personal service corporation generally must adopt a calendar year unless:

● It can establish a business purpose for having a different tax year, or

● It elects under section 444 to have a tax year other than a calendar year.

Trusts.—Generally, a trust must adopt a calendar year except for the following:

● Tax-exempt trusts,

● Charitable trusts, and

● Grantor-owned trusts.

Line 12.—If the business has or will have employees, enter the date on which the business began or will begin to pay wages. If the business does not plan to have employees, enter N/A.

Withholding agent.—Enter the date you began or will begin to pay income to a nonresident alien. This also applies to individuals who are required to file Form 1042 to report alimony paid to a nonresident alien.

Line 13.—For a definition of agricultural labor (farmworker), see **Circular A,** Agricultural Employer's Tax Guide (Publication 51).

Line 14.—Generally, enter the exact type of business being operated (for example, advertising agency, farm, food or beverage establishment, labor union, real estate agency, steam laundry, rental of coin-operated vending machine, or investment club). Also state if the business will involve the sale or distribution of alcoholic beverages.

Governmental.—Enter the type of organization (state, county, school district, municipality, etc.).

Nonprofit organization (other than governmental).—Enter whether organized for religious, educational, or humane purposes, and the principal activity (for example, religious organization—hospital, charitable).

Mining and quarrying.—Specify the process and the principal product (for example, mining bituminous coal, contract drilling for oil, or quarrying dimension stone).

Contract construction.—Specify whether general contracting or special trade contracting. Also, show the type of work normally performed (for example, general contractor for residential buildings or electrical subcontractor).

Food or beverage establishments.—Specify the type of establishment and state whether you employ workers who receive tips (for example, lounge—yes).

Trade.—Specify the type of sales and the principal line of goods sold (for example, wholesale dairy products, manufacturer's representative for mining machinery, or retail hardware).

Manufacturing.—Specify the type of establishment operated (for example, sawmill or vegetable cannery).

Signature block.—The application must be signed by (a) the individual, if the applicant is an individual, (b) the president, vice president, or other principal officer, if the applicant is a corporation, (c) a responsible and duly authorized member or officer having knowledge of its affairs, if the applicant is a partnership or other unincorporated organization, or (d) the fiduciary, if the applicant is a trust or estate.

Some Useful Publications

You may get the following publications for additional information on the subjects covered on this form. To get these and other free forms and publications, call 1-800-TAX-FORM (1-800-829-3676). You should receive your order or notification of its status within 7 to 15 workdays of your call.

Use your computer.—If you subscribe to an on-line service, ask if IRS information is available and, if so, how to access it. You can also get information through IRIS, the Internal Revenue Information Services, on FedWorld, a government bulletin board. Tax forms, instructions, publications, and other IRS information, are available through IRIS.

IRIS is accessible directly by calling 703-321-8020. On the Internet, you can telnet to fedworld.gov. or, for file transfer protocol services, connect to ftp.fedworld.gov. If you are using the WorldWide Web, connect to http://www.ustreas.gov

FedWorld's help desk offers technical assistance on accessing IRIS (not tax help) during regular business hours at 703-487-4608. The IRIS menus offer information on available file formats and software needed to read and print files. You must print the forms to use them; the forms are not designed to be filled out on-screen.

Tax forms, instructions, and publications are also available on CD-ROM, including prior-year forms starting with the 1991 tax year. For ordering information and software requirements, contact the Government Printing Office's Superintendent of Documents (202-512-1800) or Federal Bulletin Board (202-512-1387).

Pub. 1635, Understanding Your EIN

Pub. 15, Employer's Tax Guide

Pub. 15-A, Employer's Supplemental Tax Guide

Pub. 538, Accounting Periods and Methods

Pub. 541, Tax Information on Partnerships

Pub. 542, Tax Information on Corporations

Pub. 557, Tax-Exempt Status for Your Organization

Pub. 583, Starting a Business and Keeping Records

Package 1023, Application for Recognition of Exemption

Package 1024, Application for Recognition of Exemption Under Section 501(a) or for Determination Under Section 120

Paperwork Reduction Act Notice

We ask for the information on this form to carry out the Internal Revenue laws of the United States. You are required to give us the information. We need it to ensure that you are complying with these laws and to allow us to figure and collect the right amount of tax.

The time needed to complete and file this form will vary depending on individual circumstances. The estimated average time is:

Recordkeeping . . . . 7 min.

Learning about the law or the form . . . . . . 18 min.

Preparing the form . . . . . 45 min.

Copying, assembling, and sending the form to the IRS . . 20 min.

If you have comments concerning the accuracy of these time estimates or suggestions for making this form simpler, we would be happy to hear from you. You can write to the Tax Forms Committee, Western Area Distribution Center, Rancho Cordova, CA 95743-0001. **Do not** send this form to this address. Instead, see **Where To Apply** on page 2.

 Printed on recycled paper

*U.S. Government Printing Office: 1996 - 405-493/40061

Form **1040**

Department of the Treasury—Internal Revenue Service

U.S. Individual Income Tax Return (O) **1996**

IRS Use Only—Do not write or staple in this space.

For the year Jan. 1–Dec. 31, 1996, or other tax year beginning ____ , 1996, ending ____ , 19 __ | OMB No. 1545-0074

Label

(See page 11.)

Use the IRS label. Otherwise, please print or type.

L A B E L   H E R E

Your first name and initial | Last name | Your social security number

If a joint return, spouse's first name and initial | Last name | Spouse's social security number

Home address (number and street). If you have a P.O. box, see page 11. | Apt. no.

City, town or post office, state, and ZIP code. If you have a foreign address, see page 11.

For help finding line instructions, see pages 2 and 3 in the booklet.

Presidential Election Campaign

(See page 11.)

▶ Do you want $3 to go to this fund? . . . .

If a joint return, does your spouse want $3 to go to this fund? . . . .

Yes | No | **Note:** *Checking "Yes" will not change your tax or reduce your refund.*

Filing Status

Check only one box.

1 ☐ Single
2 ☐ Married filing joint return (even if only one had income)
3 ☐ Married filing separate return. Enter spouse's social security no. above and full name here. ▶ _____
4 ☐ Head of household (with qualifying person). (See instructions.) If the qualifying person is a child but not your dependent, enter this child's name here. ▶ _____
5 ☐ Qualifying widow(er) with dependent child (year spouse died ▶ 19 __). (See instructions.)

Exemptions

If more than six dependents, see the instructions for line 6c.

6a ☐ **Yourself.** If your parent (or someone else) can claim you as a dependent on his or her tax return, **do not** check box 6a . . . .

b ☐ **Spouse** . . . .

c Dependents:

(1) First name Last name	(2) Dependent's social security number. If born in Dec. 1996, see inst.	(3) Dependent's relationship to you	(4) No. of months lived in your home in 1996

d Total number of exemptions claimed . . . .

No. of boxes checked on lines 6a and 6b ____

No. of your children on line 6c who:
• lived with you ____
• did not live with you due to divorce or separation (see instructions) ____

Dependents on 6c not entered above ____

Add numbers entered on lines above ▶ ☐

Income

Attach Copy B of your Forms W-2, W-2G, and 1099-R here.

If you did not get a W-2, see the instructions for line 7.

Enclose, but do not attach, any payment. Also, please enclose **Form 1040-V** (see the instructions for line 62).

7 Wages, salaries, tips, etc. Attach Form(s) W-2 . . . . . | 7
8a **Taxable** interest. Attach Schedule B if over $400 . . . | 8a
b **Tax-exempt** interest. DO NOT include on line 8a . . | 8b |
9 Dividend income. Attach Schedule B if over $400 . . . | 9
10 Taxable refunds, credits, or offsets of state and local income taxes (see instructions) . | 10
11 Alimony received . . . . | 11
12 Business income or (loss). Attach Schedule C or C-EZ . . | 12
13 Capital gain or (loss). If required, attach Schedule D . . | 13
14 Other gains or (losses). Attach Form 4707 . . . . . | 14
15a Total IRA distributions . . | 15a | b Taxable amount (see inst.) | 15b
16a Total pensions and annuities | 16a | b Taxable amount (see inst.) | 16b
17 Rental real estate, royalties, partnerships, S corporations, trusts, etc. Attach Schedule E | 17
18 Farm income or (loss). Attach Schedule F . . . . . | 18
19 Unemployment compensation . . . . | 19
20a Social security benefits . | 20a | b Taxable amount (see inst.) | 20b
21 Other income. List type and amount—see instructions _____ | 21
22 Add the amounts in the far right column for lines 7 through 21. This is your **total income** ▶ | 22

Adjusted Gross Income

If line 31 is under $28,495 (under $9,500 if a child did not live with you), see the instructions for line 54.

23a Your IRA deduction (see instructions) . . . . . | 23a
b Spouse's IRA deduction (see instructions) . . . . | 23b
24 Moving expenses. Attach Form 3903 or 3903-F . . . | 24
25 One-half of self-employment tax. Attach Schedule SE . | 25
26 Self-employed health insurance deduction (see inst.) . | 26
27 Keogh & self-employed SEP plans. If SEP, check ▶ ☐ | 27
28 Penalty on early withdrawal of savings . . . . . | 28
29 Alimony paid. Recipient's SSN ▶ _____ | 29
30 Add lines 23a through 29 . . . . | 30
31 Subtract line 30 from line 22. This is your **adjusted gross income** ▶ | 31

For Privacy Act and Paperwork Reduction Act Notice, see page 7.

Cat. No. 11320B

Form **1040** (1996)

143

Tax Compu-tation	32	Amount from line 31 (adjusted gross income)		**32**
	33a	Check if: ☐ **You** were 65 or older, ☐ Blind; ☐ **Spouse** was 65 or older, ☐ Blind. Add the number of boxes checked above and enter the total here . . . . ▶ 33a ☐		
	b	If you are married filing separately and your spouse itemizes deductions or you were a dual-status alien, see instructions and check here . . . . . ▶ 33b ☐		
	34	Enter the **larger** of your: { **Itemized deductions** from Schedule A, line 28, **OR** **Standard deduction** shown below for your filing status. **But see the** instructions if you checked any box on line 33a or b **or** someone can claim you as a dependent. • Single—$4,000 • Married filing jointly or Qualifying widow(er)—$6,700 • Head of household—$5,900 • Married filing separately—$3,350 }		**34**
	35	Subtract line 34 from line 32		**35**
If you want the IRS to figure your tax, see the instructions for line 37.	36	If line 32 is $88,475 or less, multiply $2,550 by the total number of exemptions claimed on line 6d. If line 32 is over $88,475, see the worksheet in the inst. for the amount to enter		**36**
	37	**Taxable income.** Subtract line 36 from line 35. If line 36 is more than line 35, enter -0-		**37**
	38	**Tax.** See instructions. Check if total includes any tax from **a** ☐ Form(s) 8814 **b** ☐ Form 4972 . . . . ▶		**38**
Credits	39	Credit for child and dependent care expenses. Attach Form 2441	**39**	
	40	Credit for the elderly or the disabled. Attach Schedule R . .	**40**	
	41	Foreign tax credit. Attach Form 1116	**41**	
	42	Other. Check if from **a** ☐ Form 3800 **b** ☐ Form 8396 **c** ☐ Form 8801 **d** ☐ Form (specify) _____	**42**	
	43	Add lines 39 through 42	**43**	
	44	Subtract line 43 from line 38. If line 43 is more than line 38, enter -0- . . . . . . ▶		**44**
Other Taxes	45	Self-employment tax. Attach Schedule SE		**45**
	46	Alternative minimum tax. Attach Form 6251		**46**
	47	Social security and Medicare tax on tip income not reported to employer. Attach Form 4137 .		**47**
	48	Tax on qualified retirement plans, including IRAs. If required, attach Form 5329		**48**
	49	Advance earned income credit payments from Form(s) W-2 .		**49**
	50	Household employment taxes. Attach Schedule H		**50**
	51	Add lines 44 through 50. This is your **total tax** . . . . ▶		**51**
Payments	52	Federal income tax withheld from Forms W-2 and 1099 . .	**52**	
	53	1996 estimated tax payments and amount applied from 1995 return .	**53**	
Attach Forms W-2, W-2G, and 1099-R on the front.	54	**Earned income credit.** Attach Schedule EIC if you have a qualifying child. Nontaxable earned income: amount ▶ _____ and type ▶ _____	**54**	
	55	Amount paid with Form 4868 (request for extension) . . .	**55**	
	56	Excess social security and RRTA tax withheld (see inst.) . .	**56**	
	57	Other payments. Check if from **a** ☐ Form 2439 **b** ☐ Form 4136	**57**	
	58	Add lines 52 through 57. These are your **total payments** . . . . ▶		**58**
Refund	59	If line 58 is more than line 51, subtract line 51 from line 58. This is the amount you **OVERPAID**		**59**
Have it sent directly to your bank account! See inst. and fill in 60b, c, and d.	60a	Amount of line 59 you want **REFUNDED TO YOU** . . . . ▶		**60a**
	▶ b	Routing number _____ **c** Type: ☐ Checking ☐ Savings		
	▶ d	Account number _____		
	61	Amount of line 59 you want **APPLIED TO YOUR 1997 ESTIMATED TAX** ▶	**61**	
Amount You Owe	62	If line 51 is more than line 58, subtract line 58 from line 51. This is the **AMOUNT YOU OWE.** For details on how to pay and use **Form 1040-V**, see instructions . . . . ▶		**62**
	63	Estimated tax penalty. Also include on line 62	**63**	

Sign Here

Keep a copy of this return for your records.

Under penalties of perjury, I declare that I have examined this return and accompanying schedules and statements, and to the best of my knowledge and belief, they are true, correct, and complete. Declaration of preparer (other than taxpayer) is based on all information of which preparer has any knowledge.

▶ Your signature	Date	Your occupation
▶ Spouse's signature. If a joint return, BOTH must sign.	Date	Spouse's occupation

Paid Preparer's Use Only

Preparer's signature ▶	Date	Check if self-employed ☐	Preparer's social security no.
Firm's name (or yours if self-employed) and address ▶		EIN	
		ZIP code	

144

✪ Printed on recycled paper   *U.S. Government Printing Office: 1996 — 407-188

Form **1041**

Department of the Treasury—Internal Revenue Service

U.S. Income Tax Return for Estates and Trusts

19 96

For calendar year 1996 or fiscal year beginning _____ , 1996, and ending _____ , 19 ___

OMB No. 1545-0092

A Type of entity:	Name of estate or trust (If a grantor type trust, see page 7 of the instructions.)	**C** Employer identification number
☐ Decedent's estate		
☐ Simple trust		**D** Date entity created
☐ Complex trust	Name and title of fiduciary	**E** Nonexempt charitable and split-interest trusts, check applicable boxes (see page 8 of the instructions):
☐ Grantor type trust		
☐ Bankruptcy estate–Ch. 7		
☐ Bankruptcy estate–Ch. 11	Number, street, and room or suite no. (If a P.O. box, see page 7 of the instructions.)	☐ Described in section 4947(a)(1)
☐ Pooled income fund		☐ Not a private foundation
B Number of Schedules K-1 attached (see instructions) ▶	City or town, state, and ZIP code	☐ Described in section 4947(a)(2)

F Check applicable boxes: ☐ Initial return ☐ Final return ☐ Amended return ☐ Change in fiduciary's name ☐ Change in fiduciary's address

G Pooled mortgage account (see page 9 of the instructions): ☐ Bought ☐ Sold Date: _____

Income

1	Interest income	1
2	Dividends	2
3	Business income or (loss) (attach Schedule C or C-EZ (Form 1040))	3
4	Capital gain or (loss) (attach Schedule D (Form 1041))	4
5	Rents, royalties, partnerships, other estates and trusts, etc. (attach Schedule E (Form 1040))	5
6	Farm income or (loss) (attach Schedule F (Form 1040))	6
7	Ordinary gain or (loss) (attach Form 4797)	7
8	Other income. List type and amount _____	8
9	**Total income.** Combine lines 1 through 8 . . . . ▶	9

Deductions

10	Interest. Check if Form 4952 is attached ▶ ☐	10
11	Taxes	11
12	Fiduciary fees	12
13	Charitable deduction (from Schedule A, line 7)	13
14	Attorney, accountant, and return preparer fees	14
15a	Other deductions NOT subject to the 2% floor (attach schedule) . .	15a
b	Allowable miscellaneous itemized deductions subject to the 2% floor.	15b
16	**Total.** Add lines 10 through 15b	16
17	Adjusted total income or (loss). Subtract line 16 from line 9. Enter here and on Schedule B, line 1 ▶	17
18	Income distribution deduction (from Schedule B, line 17) (attach Schedules K-1 (Form 1041))	18
19	Estate tax deduction (including certain generation-skipping taxes) (attach computation) . .	19
20	Exemption	20
21	**Total deductions.** Add lines 18 through 20 . . . . ▶	21

Tax and Payments

22	Taxable income. Subtract line 21 from line 17. If a loss, see page 13 of the instructions	22
23	**Total tax** (from Schedule G, line 8)	23
24	**Payments: a** 1996 estimated tax payments and amount applied from 1995 return . . .	24a
b	Estimated tax payments allocated to beneficiaries (from Form 1041-T)	24b
c	Subtract line 24b from line 24a	24c
d	Tax paid with extension of time to file: ☐ Form 2758 ☐ Form 8736 ☐ Form 8800	24d
e	Federal income tax withheld. If any is from Form(s) 1099, check ▶ ☐	24e
	Other payments: **f** Form 2439 _____ ; **g** Form 4136 _____ ; Total ▶	24h
25	**Total payments.** Add lines 24c through 24e, and 24h . . . . . . ▶	25
26	Estimated tax penalty (see page 13 of the instructions)	26
27	**Tax due.** If line 25 is smaller than the total of lines 23 and 26, enter amount owed . . .	27
28	**Overpayment.** If line 25 is larger than the total of lines 23 and 26, enter amount overpaid	28
29	Amount of line 28 to be: **a Credited to 1997 estimated tax** ▶ _____ ; **b Refunded** ▶	29

Please Sign Here

Under penalties of perjury, I declare that I have examined this return, including accompanying schedules and statements, and to the best of my knowledge and belief, it is true, correct, and complete. Declaration of preparer (other than fiduciary) is based on all information of which preparer has any knowledge.

▶ _____ Date _____
Signature of fiduciary or officer representing fiduciary

▶ _____
EIN of fiduciary if a financial institution (see page 4 of the instructions)

Paid Preparer's Use Only

Preparer's signature ▶	Date	Check if self-employed ▶ ☐	Preparer's social security no.
Firm's name (or yours if self-employed) and address ▶		EIN ▶	
		ZIP code ▶	

For Paperwork Reduction Act Notice, see page 1 of the separate instructions.

Cat. No. 11370H

Form **1041** (1996)

Schedule A	Charitable Deduction. Do not complete for a simple trust or a pooled income fund.		
1	Amounts paid for charitable purposes from gross income	1	
2	Amounts permanently set aside for charitable purposes from gross income	2	
3	Add lines 1 and 2	3	
4	Tax-exempt income allocable to charitable contributions (see page 14 of the instructions) . .	4	
5	Subtract line 4 from line 3	5	
6	Capital gains for the tax year allocated to corpus and paid or permanently set aside for charitable purposes	6	
7	**Charitable deduction.** Add lines 5 and 6. Enter here and on page 1, line 13	7	

Schedule B	Income Distribution Deduction		
1	Adjusted total income (from page 1, line 17) (see page 14 of the instructions)	1	
2	Adjusted tax-exempt interest	2	
3	Total net gain from Schedule D (Form 1041), line 17, column (a) (see page 15 of the instructions)	3	
4	Enter amount from Schedule A, line 6	4	
5	Long-term capital gain for the tax year included on Schedule A, line 3	5	
6	Short-term capital gain for the tax year included on Schedule A, line 3	6	
7	If the amount on page 1, line 4, is a capital loss, enter here as a positive figure	7	
8	If the amount on page 1, line 4, is a capital gain, enter here as a negative figure	8	
9	**Distributable net income (DNI).** Combine lines 1 through 8. If zero or less, enter -0-	9	
10	If a complex trust, enter accounting income for the tax year as determined under the governing instrument and applicable local law **10**		
11	Income required to be distributed currently	11	
12	Other amounts paid, credited, or otherwise required to be distributed	12	
13	Total distributions. Add lines 11 and 12. If greater than line 10, see page 15 of the instructions	13	
14	Enter the amount of tax-exempt income included on line 13	14	
15	Tentative income distribution deduction. Subtract line 14 from line 13	15	
16	Tentative income distribution deduction. Subtract line 2 from line 9. If zero or less, enter -0-	16	
17	**Income distribution deduction.** Enter the smaller of line 15 or line 16 here and on page 1, line 18	17	

Schedule G	Tax Computation (see page 16 of the instructions)		
1	**Tax: a** ☐ Tax rate schedule or ☐ Schedule D (Form 1041) . .	1a	
	b Other taxes	1b	
	c Total. Add lines 1a and 1b. . . . . ▶	1c	
2a	Foreign tax credit (attach Form 1116)	2a	
b	Check: ☐ Nonconventional source fuel credit ☐ Form 8834 . . .	2b	
c	General business credit. Enter here and check which forms are attached: ☐ Form 3800 or ☐ Forms (specify) ▶	2c	
d	Credit for prior year minimum tax (attach Form 8801)	2d	
3	**Total credits.** Add lines 2a through 2d . . . . ▶	3	
4	Subtract line 3 from line 1c	4	
5	Recapture taxes. Check if from: ☐ Form 4255 ☐ Form 8611. . .	5	
6	Alternative minimum tax (from Schedule I, line 41).	6	
7	Household employment taxes. Attach Schedule H (Form 1040) . . .	7	
8	**Total tax.** Add lines 4 through 7. Enter here and on page 1, line 23 . ▶	8	

Other Information

		Yes	No
1	Did the estate or trust receive tax-exempt income? If "Yes," attach a computation of the allocation of expenses. Enter the amount of tax-exempt interest income and exempt-interest dividends ▶ $ ----------------------------		
2	Did the estate or trust receive all or any part of the earnings (salary, wages, and other compensation) of any individual by reason of a contract assignment or similar arrangement?		
3	At any time during calendar year 1996, did the estate or trust have an interest in or a signature or other authority over a bank, securities, or other financial account in a foreign country? See page 17 of the instructions for exceptions and filing requirements for Form TD F 90-22.1. If "Yes," enter the name of the foreign country ▶ ----------------------------		
4	During the tax year, did the estate or trust receive a distribution from, or was it the grantor of, or transferor to, a foreign trust? If "Yes," see page 17 of the instructions for other forms the estate or trust may have to file		
5	Did the estate or trust receive, or pay, any seller-financed mortgage interest? If "Yes," see page 17 of the instructions for required attachment		
6	If this is a complex trust making the section 663(b) election, check here (see page 17 of the instructions) ▶ ☐		
7	To make a section 643(e)(3) election, attach Schedule D (Form 1041), and check here (see page 17). . ▶ ☐		
8	If the decedent's estate has been open for more than 2 years, check here . . . . ▶ ☐		

146

Schedule I   **Alternative Minimum Tax** (see pages 18 through 22 of the instructions)

Part I—Estate's or Trust's Share of Alternative Minimum Taxable Income

1	Adjusted total income or (loss) (from page 1, line 17)	**1**
2	Net operating loss deduction. Enter as a positive amount	**2**
3	Add lines 1 and 2	**3**

4   **Adjustments and tax preference items:**

a	Interest	**4a**
b	Taxes	**4b**
c	Miscellaneous itemized deductions (from page 1, line 15b)	**4c**
d	Refund of taxes	**4d** ( )
e	Depreciation of property placed in service after 1986	**4e**
f	Circulation and research and experimental expenditures	**4f**
g	Mining exploration and development costs	**4g**
h	Long-term contracts entered into after February 28, 1986	**4h**
i	Amortization of pollution control facilities	**4i**
j	Installment sales of certain property	**4j**
k	Adjusted gain or loss (including incentive stock options).	**4k**
l	Certain loss limitations	**4l**
m	Tax shelter farm activities	**4m**
n	Passive activities	**4n**
o	Beneficiaries of other trusts or decedent's estates	**4o**
p	Tax-exempt interest from specified private activity bonds	**4p**
q	Depletion	**4q**
r	Accelerated depreciation of real property placed in service before 1987	**4r**
s	Accelerated depreciation of leased personal property placed in service before 1987	**4s**
t	Intangible drilling costs	**4t**
u	Other adjustments	**4u**

5	Combine lines 4a through 4u	**5**
6	Add lines 3 and 5	**6**
7	Alternative tax net operating loss deduction (see page 21 of the instructions for limitations). .	**7**
8	Adjusted alternative minimum taxable income. Subtract line 7 from line 6. Enter here and on line 13	**8**

Note: *Complete Part II before going to line 9.*

9	Income distribution deduction from line 27	**9**
10	Estate tax deduction (from page 1, line 19)	**10**
11	Add lines 9 and 10	**11**
12	Estate's or trust's share of alternative minimum taxable income. Subtract line 11 from line 8 .	**12**

If line 12 is:

- $22,500 or less, stop here and enter -0- on Schedule G, line 6. The estate or trust is not liable for the alternative minimum tax.
- Over $22,500, but less than $165,000, go to line 28.
- $165,000 or more, enter the amount from line 12 on line 34 and go to line 35.

(continued on page 4)

Part II—Income Distribution Deduction on a Minimum Tax Basis

13	Adjusted alternative minimum taxable income (from line 8)	13	
14	Adjusted tax-exempt interest (other than amounts included on line 4p).	14	
15	Total net gain from Schedule D (Form 1041), line 17, column (a). If a loss, enter -0-	15	
16	Capital gains for the tax year allocated to corpus and paid or permanently set aside for charitable purposes (from Schedule A, line 6)	16	
17	Capital gains paid or permanently set aside for charitable purposes from current year's income (see page 21 of the instructions).	17	
18	Capital gains computed on a minimum tax basis included on line 8	18 (	)
19	Capital losses computed on a minimum tax basis included on line 8. Enter as a positive amount	19	
20	Distributable net alternative minimum taxable income (DNAMTI). Combine lines 13 through 19 .	20	
21	Income required to be distributed currently (from Schedule B, line 11)	21	
22	Other amounts paid, credited, or otherwise required to be distributed (from Schedule B, line 12)	22	
23	Total distributions. Add lines 21 and 22	23	
24	Tax-exempt income included on line 23 (other than amounts included on line 4p)	24	
25	Tentative income distribution deduction on a minimum tax basis. Subtract line 24 from line 23 .	25	
26	Tentative income distribution deduction on a minimum tax basis. Subtract line 14 from line 20 .	26	
27	**Income distribution deduction on a minimum tax basis.** Enter the smaller of line 25 or line 26. Enter here and on line 9	27	

Part III—Alternative Minimum Tax

28	Exemption amount		28	$22,500
29	Enter the amount from line 12	29		
30	Phase-out of exemption amount	30	$75,000	
31	Subtract line 30 from line 29. If zero or less, enter -0- . . .	31		
32	Multiply line 31 by 25% (.25)		32	
33	Subtract line 32 from line 28. If zero or less, enter -0-		33	
34	Subtract line 33 from line 29		34	
35	If line 34 is:			
	• $175,000 or less, multiply line 34 by 26% (.26).			
	• Over $175,000, multiply line 34 by 28% (.28) and subtract $3,500 from the result		35	
36	Alternative minimum foreign tax credit (see page 21 of instructions).		36	
37	Tentative minimum tax. Subtract line 36 from line 35		37	
38	Regular tax before credits (see page 22 of instructions)	38		
39	Section 644 tax included on Schedule G, line 1b	39		
40	Add lines 38 and 39		40	
41	**Alternative minimum tax.** Subtract line 40 from line 37. If zero or less, enter -0-. Enter here and on Schedule G, line 6		41	

✿ *Printed on recycled paper*

Form **706**	**United States Estate (and Generation-Skipping Transfer) Tax Return**		
(Rev. April 1997)	Estate of a citizen or resident of the United States (see separate instructions). To be filed for decedents dying after October 8, 1990. For Paperwork Reduction Act Notice, see page 1 of the separate instructions.		OMB No. 1545-0015
Department of the Treasury Internal Revenue Service			

Part 1.—Decedent and Executor

1a Decedent's first name and middle initial (and maiden name, if any)	1b Decedent's last name	2 Decedent's social security no.

3a Legal residence (domicile) at time of death (county, state, and ZIP code, or foreign country)	3b Year domicile established	4 Date of birth	5 Date of death

6a Name of executor (see page 2 of the instructions)	6b Executor's address (number and street including apartment or suite no. or rural route; city, town, or post office; state; and ZIP code)

6c Executor's social security number (see page 2 of the instructions)

7a Name and location of court where will was probated or estate administered	7b Case number

8 If decedent died testate, check here ▶ ☐ and attach a certified copy of the will. **9** If Form 4768 is attached, check here ▶ ☐

10 If Schedule R-1 is attached, check here ▶ ☐

Part 2.—Tax Computation

1	Total gross estate (from Part 5, Recapitulation, page 3, item 10)	1	
2	Total allowable deductions (from Part 5, Recapitulation, page 3, item 20)	2	
3	Taxable estate (subtract line 2 from line 1)	3	
4	Adjusted taxable gifts (total taxable gifts (within the meaning of section 2503) made by the decedent after December 31, 1976, other than gifts that are includible in decedent's gross estate (section 2001(b)))	4	
5	Add lines 3 and 4	5	
6	Tentative tax on the amount on line 5 from Table A on page 10 of the instructions	6	
7a	If line 5 exceeds $10,000,000, enter the lesser of line 5 or $21,040,000. If line 5 is $10,000,000 or less, skip lines 7a and 7b and enter -0- on line 7c .	7a	
b	Subtract $10,000,000 from line 7a	7b	
c	Enter 5% (.05) of line 7b	7c	
8	Total tentative tax (add lines 6 and 7c)	8	
9	Total gift tax payable with respect to gifts made by the decedent after December 31, 1976. Include gift taxes by the decedent's spouse for such spouse's share of split gifts (section 2513) only if the decedent was the donor of these gifts and they are includible in the decedent's gross estate (see instructions)	9	
10	Gross estate tax (subtract line 9 from line 8)	10	
11	Maximum unified credit against estate tax	11	192,800 00
12	Adjustment to unified credit. (This adjustment may not exceed $6,000. See page 7 of the instructions.)	12	
13	Allowable unified credit (subtract line 12 from line 11)	13	
14	Subtract line 13 from line 10 (but do not enter less than zero)	14	
15	Credit for state death taxes. Do not enter more than line 14. Figure the credit by using the amount on line 3 less $60,000. See Table B in the instructions and **attach credit evidence** (see instructions) .	15	
16	Subtract line 15 from line 14	16	
17	Credit for Federal gift taxes on pre-1977 gifts (section 2012) (attach computation)	17	
18	Credit for foreign death taxes (from Schedule(s) P). (Attach Form(s) 706-CE.)	18	
19	Credit for tax on prior transfers (from Schedule Q)	19	
20	Total (add lines 17, 18, and 19)	20	
21	Net estate tax (subtract line 20 from line 16)	21	
22	Generation-skipping transfer taxes (from Schedule R, Part 2, line 10)	22	
23	Section 4980A increased estate tax (from Schedule S, Part I, line 17) (see page 20 of the instructions)	23	
24	Total transfer taxes (add lines 21, 22, and 23)	24	
25	Prior payments. Explain in an attached statement	25	
26	United States Treasury bonds redeemed in payment of estate tax . .	26	
27	Total (add lines 25 and 26).	27	
28	Balance due (or overpayment) (subtract line 27 from line 24)	28	

Under penalties of perjury, I declare that I have examined this return, including accompanying schedules and statements, and to the best of my knowledge and belief, it is true, correct, and complete. Declaration of preparer other than the executor is based on all information of which preparer has any knowledge.

Signature(s) of executor(s) _____ Date _____

Signature of preparer other than executor _____ Address (and ZIP code) _____ Date _____

Cat. No. 20548R

149

Form 706 (Rev. 4-97)

Estate of:

Part 3.—Elections by the Executor

Please check the "Yes" or "No" box for each question. (See instructions beginning on page 3.) | Yes | No

1 Do you elect alternate valuation? . . . .

2 Do you elect special use valuation? . . . .
If "Yes," you must complete and attach Schedule A–1.

3 Do you elect to pay the taxes in installments as described in section 6166? . . . .
If "Yes," you must attach the additional information described on page 5 of the instructions.

4 Do you elect to postpone the part of the taxes attributable to a reversionary or remainder interest as described in section 6163? . . . .

Part 4.—General Information (Note: *Please attach the necessary supplemental documents.* **You must attach the death certificate.**)
(See instructions beginning on page 6.)

Authorization to receive confidential tax information under Regulations section 601.504(b)(2)(i), to act as the estate's representative before the Internal Revenue Service, and to make written or oral presentations on behalf of the estate if return prepared by an attorney, accountant, or enrolled agent for the executor:

Name of representative (print or type)	State	Address (number, street, and room or suite no., city, state, and ZIP code)

I declare that I am the ☐ attorney/ ☐ certified public accountant/ ☐ enrolled agent (you must check the applicable box) for the executor and prepared this return for the executor. I am not under suspension or disbarment from practice before the Internal Revenue Service and am qualified to practice in the state shown above.

Signature	CAF number	Date	Telephone number

1 Death certificate number and issuing authority (attach a copy of the death certificate to this return).

2 Decedent's business or occupation. If retired, check here ▶ ☐ and state decedent's former business or occupation.

3 Marital status of the decedent at time of death:
☐ Married
☐ Widow or widower—Name, SSN, and date of death of deceased spouse ▶
☐ Single
☐ Legally separated
☐ Divorced—Date divorce decree became final ▶

4a Surviving spouse's name	4b Social security number	4c Amount received (see page 6 of the instructions)

5 Individuals (other than the surviving spouse), trusts, or other estates who receive benefits from the estate (do not include charitable beneficiaries shown in Schedule O) (see instructions). For Privacy Act Notice (applicable to individual beneficiaries only), see the Instructions for Form 1040.

Name of individual, trust, or estate receiving $5,000 or more	Identifying number	Relationship to decedent	Amount (see instructions)

All unascertainable beneficiaries and those who receive less than $5,000 . . . . ▶

Total . . . .

(continued on next page)

150

Page 2

Part 4.—General Information (continued)

		Yes	No
	Please check the "Yes" or "No" box for each question.		
6	Does the gross estate contain any section 2044 property (qualified terminable interest property (QTIP) from a prior gift or estate) (see page 6 of the instructions)?		
7a	Have Federal gift tax returns ever been filed?		
	If "Yes," please attach copies of the returns, if available, and furnish the following information:		

7b Period(s) covered	7c Internal Revenue office(s) where filed

If you answer "Yes" to any of questions 8–16, you must attach additional information as described in the instructions.

		Yes	No
8a	Was there any insurance on the decedent's life that is not included on the return as part of the gross estate?		
b	Did the decedent own any insurance on the life of another that is not included in the gross estate?		
9	Did the decedent at the time of death own any property as a joint tenant with right of survivorship in which (a) one or more of the other joint tenants was someone other than the decedent's spouse, and (b) less than the full value of the property is included on the return as part of the gross estate? If "Yes," you must complete and attach Schedule E		
10	Did the decedent, at the time of death, own any interest in a partnership or unincorporated business or any stock in an inactive or closely held corporation?		
11	Did the decedent make any transfer described in section 2035, 2036, 2037, or 2038 (see the instructions for Schedule G beginning on page 11 of the separate instructions)? If "Yes," you must complete and attach Schedule G		
12	Were there in existence at the time of the decedent's death:		
a	Any trusts created by the decedent during his or her lifetime?		
b	Any trusts not created by the decedent under which the decedent possessed any power, beneficial interest, or trusteeship?		
13	Did the decedent ever possess, exercise, or release any general power of appointment? If "Yes," you must complete and attach Schedule H		
14	Was the marital deduction computed under the transitional rule of Public Law 97-34, section 403(e)(3) (Economic Recovery Tax Act of 1981)? If "Yes," attach a separate computation of the marital deduction, enter the amount on item 18 of the Recapitulation, and note on item 18 "computation attached."		
15	Was the decedent, immediately before death, receiving an annuity described in the "General" paragraph of the instructions for Schedule I? If "Yes," you must complete and attach Schedule I		
16	Did the decedent have a total "excess retirement accumulation" (as defined in section 4980A(d)) in qualified employer plans and individual retirement plans? If "Yes," you must complete and attach Schedule S		

Part 5.—Recapitulation

Item number	Gross estate	Alternate value	Value at date of death
1	Schedule A—Real Estate		
2	Schedule B—Stocks and Bonds		
3	Schedule C—Mortgages, Notes, and Cash		
4	Schedule D—Insurance on the Decedent's Life (attach Form(s) 712)		
5	Schedule E—Jointly Owned Property (attach Form(s) 712 for life insurance) . . .		
6	Schedule F—Other Miscellaneous Property (attach Form(s) 712 for life insurance) .		
7	Schedule G—Transfers During Decedent's Life (attach Form(s) 712 for life insurance)		
8	Schedule H—Powers of Appointment		
9	Schedule I—Annuities		
10	Total gross estate (add items 1 through 9). Enter here and on line 1 of the Tax Computation		

Item number	Deductions	Amount
11	Schedule J—Funeral Expenses and Expenses Incurred in Administering Property Subject to Claims . . .	
12	Schedule K—Debts of the Decedent	
13	Schedule K—Mortgages and Liens	
14	Total of items 11 through 13	
15	Allowable amount of deductions from item 14 (see the instructions for item 15 of the Recapitulation) . . .	
16	Schedule L—Net Losses During Administration	
17	Schedule L—Expenses Incurred in Administering Property Not Subject to Claims	
18	Schedule M—Bequests, etc., to Surviving Spouse	
19	Schedule O—Charitable, Public, and Similar Gifts and Bequests	
20	Total allowable deductions (add items 15 through 19). Enter here and on line 2 of the Tax Computation . .	

Page 3

Estate of:

SCHEDULE A—Real Estate

- *For jointly owned property that must be disclosed on Schedule E, see the instructions on the reverse side of Schedule E.*
- *Real estate that is part of a sole proprietorship should be shown on Schedule F.*
- *Real estate that is included in the gross estate under section 2035, 2036, 2037, or 2038 should be shown on Schedule G.*
- *Real estate that is included in the gross estate under section 2041 should be shown on Schedule H.*
- *If you elect section 2032A valuation, you must complete Schedule A and Schedule A-1.*

Item number	Description	Alternate valuation date	Alternate value	Value at date of death
1				
	Total from continuation schedules or additional sheets attached to this schedule . . .			
	TOTAL. (Also enter on Part 5, Recapitulation, page 3, at item 1.)			

(If more space is needed, attach the continuation schedule from the end of this package or additional sheets of the same size.)

(See the instructions on the reverse side.)

Schedule A— Page 4

Form **709**
(Rev. December 1996)

Department of the Treasury
Internal Revenue Service

United States Gift (and Generation-Skipping Transfer) Tax Return

(Section 6019 of the Internal Revenue Code) (For gifts made after December 31, 1991)

Calendar year 19 ....

▶ **See separate instructions. For Privacy Act Notice, see the Instructions for Form 1040.**

OMB No. 1545-0020

Part 1—General Information

1 Donor's first name and middle initial	2 Donor's last name	3 **Donor's social security number**

4 Address (number, street, and apartment number)	5 Legal residence (domicile) (county and state)

6 City, state, and ZIP code	7 Citizenship

		Yes	No
8	If the donor died during the year, check here ▶ ☐ and enter date of death................... , ...		
9	If you received an extension of time to file this Form 709, check here ▶ ☐ and attach the Form 4868, 2688, 2350, or extension letter		
10	Enter the total number of separate donees listed on Schedule A—count each person only once. ▶		
11a	Have you (the donor) previously filed a Form 709 (or 709-A) for any other year? If the answer is "No," do not complete line 11b .		
11b	If the answer to line 11a is "Yes," has your address changed since you last filed Form 709 (or 709-A)?		
12	Gifts by husband or wife to third parties.—Do you consent to have the gifts (including generation-skipping transfers) made by you and by your spouse to third parties during the calendar year considered as made one-half by each of you? (See instructions.) (If the answer is "Yes," the following information must be furnished and your spouse must sign the consent shown below. **If the answer is "No," skip lines 13–18 and go to Schedule A.**)		

13 Name of consenting spouse	14 SSN		

15	Were you married to one another during the entire calendar year? (see instructions)		
16	If the answer to 15 is "No," check whether ☐ married ☐ divorced or ☐ widowed, and give date (see instructions) ▶		
17	Will a gift tax return for this calendar year be filed by your spouse?		
18	**Consent of Spouse**—I consent to have the gifts (and generation-skipping transfers) made by me and by my spouse to third parties during the calendar year considered as made one-half by each of us. We are both aware of the joint and several liability for tax created by the execution of this consent.		

Consenting spouse's signature ▶

Date ▶

Part 2—Tax Computation

1	Enter the amount from Schedule A, Part 3, line 15	1	
2	Enter the amount from Schedule B, line 3	2	
3	Total taxable gifts (add lines 1 and 2)	3	
4	Tax computed on amount on line 3 (see Table for Computing Tax in separate instructions). . .	4	
5	Tax computed on amount on line 2 (see Table for Computing Tax in separate instructions). . .	5	
6	Balance (subtract line 5 from line 4)	6	
7	Maximum unified credit (nonresident aliens, see instructions)	7	192,800	00
8	Enter the unified credit against tax allowable for all prior periods (from Sch. B, line 1, col. C) . .	8	
9	Balance (subtract line 8 from line 7)	9	
10	Enter 20% (.20) of the amount allowed as a specific exemption for gifts made after September 8, 1976, and before January 1, 1977 (see instructions)	10	
11	Balance (subtract line 10 from line 9)	11	
12	Unified credit (enter the smaller of line 6 or line 11)	12	
13	Credit for foreign gift taxes (see instructions)	13	
14	Total credits (add lines 12 and 13)	14	
15	Balance (subtract line 14 from line 6) (do not enter less than zero)	15	
16	Generation-skipping transfer taxes (from Schedule C, Part 3, col. H, Total)	16	
17	Total tax (add lines 15 and 16)	17	
18	Gift and generation-skipping transfer taxes prepaid with extension of time to file	18	
19	If line 18 is less than line 17, enter BALANCE DUE (see instructions)	19	
20	If line 18 is greater than line 17, enter AMOUNT TO BE REFUNDED	20	

Under penalties of perjury, I declare that I have examined this return, including any accompanying schedules and statements, and to the best of my knowledge and belief it is true, correct, and complete. Declaration of preparer (other than donor) is based on all information of which preparer has any knowledge.

Donor's signature ▶

Date ▶

Preparer's signature (other than donor) ▶

Date ▶

Preparer's address (other than donor) ▶

Attach check or money order here.

For Paperwork Reduction Act Notice, see page 1 of the separate instructions for this form.

Cat. No. 16783M

Form **709** (Rev. 12-96)

153

SCHEDULE A   **Computation of Taxable Gifts**

Does the value of any item listed on Schedule A reflect any valuation discount? If the answer is "Yes," see instructions   . . .Yes ☐ No ☐

Part 1—Gifts Subject Only to Gift Tax. *Gifts less political organization, medical, and educational exclusions—see instructions*

A Item number	B • Donee's name and address • Relationship to donor (if any) • Description of gift • If the gift was made by means of a trust, enter trust's identifying number and attach a copy of the trust instrument • If the gift was of securities, give CUSIP number	C Donor's adjusted basis of gift	D Date of gift	E Value at date of gift
1				

Total of Part 1 (add amounts from Part 1, column E) . . . . ▶

Part 2—Gifts That are Direct Skips and are Subject to Both Gift Tax and Generation-Skipping Transfer Tax. You must list the gifts in chronological order. *Gifts less political organization, medical, and educational exclusions—see instructions. (Also list here direct skips that are subject only to the GST tax at this time as the result of the termination of an "estate tax inclusion period." See instructions.)*

A Item number	B • Donee's name and address • Relationship to donor (if any) • Description of gift • If the gift was made by means of a trust, enter trust's identifying number and attach a copy of the trust instrument • If the gift was of securities, give CUSIP number	C Donor's adjusted basis of gift	D Date of gift	E Value at date of gift
1				

Total of Part 2 (add amounts from Part 2, column E) . . . . ▶

Part 3—Taxable Gift Reconciliation

1	Total value of gifts of donor (add totals from column E of Parts 1 and 2)	**1**		
2	One-half of items ....attributable to spouse (see instructions)	**2**		
3	Balance (subtract line 2 from line 1)	**3**		
4	Gifts of spouse to be included (from Schedule A, Part 3, line 2 of spouse's return—see instructions) . .	**4**		

If any of the gifts included on this line are also subject to the generation-skipping transfer tax, check here ▶ ☐   and enter those gifts also on Schedule C, Part 1.

5	Total gifts (add lines 3 and 4)	**5**		
6	Total annual exclusions for gifts listed on Schedule A (including line 4, above) (see instructions) . . .	**6**		
7	Total included amount of gifts (subtract line 6 from line 5)	**7**		

Deductions (see instructions)

8	Gifts of interests to spouse for which a marital deduction will be claimed, based on items .... of Schedule A	**8**			
9	Exclusions attributable to gifts on line 8	**9**			
10	Marital deduction—subtract line 9 from line 8	**10**			
11	Charitable deduction, based on items ....less exclusions . .	**11**			
12	Total deductions—add lines 10 and 11			**12**	
13	Subtract line 12 from line 7			**13**	
14	Generation-skipping transfer taxes payable with this Form 709 (from Schedule C, Part 3, col. H, Total) .			**14**	
15	Taxable gifts (add lines 13 and 14). Enter here and on line 1 of the Tax Computation on page 1 . . .			**15**	

(If more space is needed, attach additional sheets of same size.)

154

SCHEDULE A	Computation of Taxable Gifts *(continued)*

16 Terminable Interest (QTIP) Marital Deduction. (See instructions for line 8 of Schedule A.)

If a trust (or other property) meets the requirements of qualified terminable interest property under section 2523(f), and

    a. The trust (or other property) is listed on Schedule A, and

    b. The value of the trust (or other property) is entered in whole or in part as a deduction on line 8, Part 3 of Schedule A,

then the donor shall be deemed to have made an election to have such trust (or other property) treated as qualified terminable interest property under section 2523(f).

If less than the entire value of the trust (or other property) that the donor has included in Part 1 of Schedule A is entered as a deduction on line 8, the donor shall be considered to have made an election only as to a fraction of the trust (or other property). The numerator of this fraction is equal to the amount of the trust (or other property) deducted on line 10 of Part 3, Schedule A. The denominator is equal to the total value of the trust (or other property) listed in Part 1 of Schedule A.

If you make the QTIP election (see instructions for line 8 of Schedule A), the terminable interest property involved will be included in your spouse's gross estate upon his or her death (section 2044). If your spouse disposes (by gift or otherwise) of all or part of the qualifying life income interest, he or she will be considered to have made a transfer of the entire property that is subject to the gift tax (see Transfer of Certain Life Estates on page 3 of the instructions).

17 Election Out of QTIP Treatment of Annuities

☐ ◄ Check here if you elect under section 2523(f)(6) **NOT** to treat as qualified terminable interest property any joint and survivor annuities that are reported on Schedule A and would otherwise be treated as qualified terminable interest property under section 2523(f). (See instructions.)
Enter the item numbers (from Schedule A) for the annuities for which you are making this election ► _____

SCHEDULE B	Gifts From Prior Periods

If you answered "Yes" on line 11a of page 1, Part 1, see the instructions for completing Schedule B. If you answered "No," skip to the Tax Computation on page 1 (or Schedule C, if applicable).

A Calendar year or calendar quarter (see instructions)	B Internal Revenue office where prior return was filed	C Amount of unified credit against gift tax for periods after December 31, 1976	D Amount of specific exemption for prior periods ending before January 1, 1977	E Amount of taxable gifts

1	Totals for prior periods (without adjustment for reduced specific exemption)	**1**			
2	Amount, if any, by which total specific exemption, line 1, column D, is more than $30,000		**2**		
3	Total amount of taxable gifts for prior periods (add amount, column E, line 1, and amount, if any, on line 2). (Enter here and on line 2 of the Tax Computation on page 1.)		**3**		

(If more space is needed, attach additional sheets of same size.)

155

SCHEDULE C   Computation of Generation-Skipping Transfer Tax

Note: *Inter vivos direct skips that are completely excluded by the GST exemption must still be fully reported (including value and exemptions claimed) on Schedule C.*

Part 1—Generation-Skipping Transfers

A Item No. (from Schedule A, Part 2, col. A)	B Value (from Schedule A, Part 2, col. E)	C Split Gifts (enter ½ of col. B) (see instructions)	D Subtract col. C from col. B	E Nontaxable portion of transfer	F Net Transfer (subtract col. E from col. D)
1					
2					
3					
4					
5					
6					

If you elected gift splitting and your spouse was required to file a separate Form 709 (see the instructions for "Split Gifts"), you must enter all of the gifts shown on Schedule A, Part 2, of your spouse's Form 709 here.	Split gifts from spouse's Form 709 (enter item number)	Value included from spouse's Form 709	Nontaxable portion of transfer	Net transfer (subtract col. E from col. D)
In column C, enter the item number of each gift in the order it appears in column A of your spouse's Schedule A, Part 2. We have preprinted the prefix "S-" to distinguish your spouse's item numbers from your own when you complete column A of Schedule C, Part 3.	S-			
	S-			
	S-			
	S-			
	S-			
In column D, for each gift, enter the amount reported in column C, Schedule C, Part 1, of your spouse's Form 709.	S-			
	S-			
	S-			

Part 2—GST Exemption Reconciliation (Section 2631) and Section 2652(a)(3) Election

Check box ▶ ☐ if you are making a section 2652(a)(3) (special QTIP) election (see instructions)

Enter the item numbers (from Schedule A) of the gifts for which you are making this election ▶ ....

1	Maximum allowable exemption	1	$1,000,000
2	Total exemption used for periods before filing this return	2	
3	Exemption available for this return (subtract line 2 from line 1)	3	
4	Exemption claimed on this return (from Part 3, col. C total, below)	4	
5	Exemption allocated to transfers not shown on Part 3, below. **You must attach a Notice of Allocation.** (See instructions.)	5	
6	Add lines 4 and 5	6	
7	Exemption available for future transfers (subtract line 6 from line 3)	7	

Part 3—Tax Computation

A Item No. (from Schedule C, Part 1)	B Net transfer (from Schedule C, Part 1, col. F)	C GST Exemption Allocated	D Divide col. C by col. B	E Inclusion Ratio (subtract col. D from 1.000)	F Maximum Estate Tax Rate	G Applicable Rate (multiply col. E by col. F)	H Generation-Skipping Transfer Tax (multiply col. B by col. G)
1					55% (.55)		
2					55% (.55)		
3					55% (.55)		
4					55% (.55)		
5					55% (.55)		
6					55% (.55)		
					55% (.55)		
					55% (.55)		
					55% (.55)		
					55% (.55)		

Total exemption claimed. Enter here and on line 4, Part 2, above. May not exceed line 3, Part 2, above		**Total generation-skipping transfer tax.** Enter here, on line 14 of Schedule A, Part 3, and on line 16 of the Tax Computation on page 1	

(If more space is needed, attach additional sheets of same size.)   ✪ **Printed on recycled paper**   *U.S. Government Printing Office: 1997 — 417-677/60033*

INDEX

Your #1 Source for Real World Legal Information...

Sphinx® Publishing
A Division of Sourcebooks, Inc.

- Written by lawyers
- Simple English explanation of the law
- Forms and instructions included

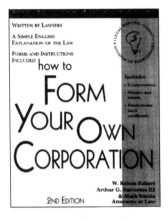

HOW TO FILE YOUR OWN BANKRUPTCY, 4TH EDITION

Whether you are considering filing for bankruptcy or are looking to avoid it at all costs, this book can help you. Includes instructions and forms necessary for filing Chapter 7 (debt discharge) and Chapter 13 (payment plan) bankruptcy and much more!

208 pages; $19.95;
ISBN 1-57071-223-9

HOW TO FILE YOUR OWN DIVORCE, 3RD EDITION

Step-by-step guide for filing for divorce in all 50 states and the District of Columbia with forms. Explains all aspects of divorce including child custody, child support, alimony, and what to do if you can't find your spouse.

256 pages; $19.95;
ISBN 1-57071-224-7

HOW TO FORM YOUR OWN CORPORATION, 2ND EDITION

Protect yourself from personal liability by incorporating your business. Contains a summary of the laws and forms with instructions for forming a corporation in all 50 states and the District of Columbia. Saves entrepreneurs precious capital!

314 pages; $14.95;
ISBN 1-57071-337-5

See the following order form for books written specifically for California, Florida, Georgia, Illinois, Massachusetts, Michigan, Minnesota, New York, North Carolina, Pennsylvania, and Texas! *Coming in 1999: Ohio!*

What our customers say about our books:

"It couldn't be more clear for the lay person." —R.D.

"I want you to know I really appreciate your book. It has saved me a lot of time and money." —L.T.

"Your real estate contracts book has saved me nearly $12,000.00 in closing costs over the past year." —A.B.

"...many of the legal questions that I have had over the years were answered clearly and concisely through your plain English interpretation of the law." —C.E.H.

"If there weren't people out there like you I'd be lost. You have the best books of this type out there." —S.B.

"...your forms and directions are easy to follow." —C.V.M.

Sphinx Publishing's Legal Survival Guides
are directly available from the Sourcebooks, Inc., or from your local bookstores.
For credit card orders call 1–800–43–BRIGHT, write P.O. Box 372, Naperville, IL 60566,
or fax 630-961-2168

Sphinx® Publishing National Titles
Valid in All 50 States

Legal Survival in Business

How to Form Your Own Corporation (2E)	$19.95
How to Form Your Own Partnership	$19.95
How to Register Your Own Copyright (2E)	$19.95
How to Register Your Own Trademark (2E)	$19.95
Most Valuable Business Legal Forms You'll Ever Need (2E)	$19.95
Most Valuable Corporate Forms You'll Ever Need (2E)	$24.95
Software Law (with diskette)	$29.95

Legal Survival in Court

Crime Victim's Guide to Justice	$19.95
Debtors' Rights (3E)	$12.95
Defend Yourself Against Criminal Charges	$19.95
Grandparents' Rights	$19.95
Help Your Lawyer Win Your Case	$12.95
Jurors' Rights (2E)	$9.95
Legal Malpractice and Other Claims Against Your Lawyer	$18.95
Legal Research Made Easy (2E)	$14.95
Simple Ways to Protect Yourself From Lawsuits	$24.95
Victims' Rights	$12.95
Winning Your Personal Injury Claim	$19.95

Legal Survival in Real Estate

How to Buy a Condominium or Townhome	$16.95
How to Negotiate Real Estate Contracts (3E)	$16.95
How to Negotiate Real Estate Leases (3E)	$16.95
Successful Real Estate Brokerage Management	$19.95

Legal Survival in Personal Affairs

How to File Your Own Bankruptcy (4E)	$19.95
How to File Your Own Divorce (3E)	$19.95
How to Make Your Own Will	$12.95
How to Write Your Own Living Will	$9.95
How to Write Your Own Premarital Agreement (2E)	$19.95
How to Win Your Unemployment Compensation Claim	$19.95
Living Trusts and Simple Ways to Avoid Probate (2E)	$19.95
Most Valuable Personal Legal Forms You'll Ever Need	$14.95
Neighbor vs. Neighbor	$12.95
The Power of Attorney Handbook (3E)	$19.95
Simple Ways to Protect Yourself from Lawsuits	$24.95
Social Security Benefits Handbook (2E)	$14.95
Unmarried Parents' Rights	$19.95
U.S.A. Immigration Guide (3E)	$19.95
Guia de Inmigracion a Estados Unidos	$19.95

Sphinx Publishing's Legal Survival Guides
are directly available from Sourcebooks, Inc., or from your local bookstores.
For credit card orders call 1–800–43-BRIGHT, write P.O. Box 372, Naperville, IL 60566,
or fax 630-961-2168

SPHINX® PUBLISHING ORDER FORM

BILL TO:		SHIP TO:	
Phone #	Terms	F.O.B. Chicago, IL	Ship Date

Charge my: ☐ VISA ☐ MasterCard ☐ American Express

☐ **Money Order or Personal Check**

Credit Card Number

Expiration Date

Qty	ISBN	Title	Retail	Ext.
		SPHINX® PUBLISHING NATIONAL TITLES		
	1-57071-166-6	Crime Victim's Guide to Justice	$19.95	
	1-57071-342-1	Debtors' Rights (3E)	$12.95	
	1-57071-162-3	Defend Yourself against Criminal Charges	$19.95	
	1-57248-001-7	Grandparents' Rights	$19.95	
	0-913825-99-9	Guia de Inmigracion a Estados Unidos	$19.95	
	1-57248-021-1	Help Your Lawyer Win Your Case	$12.95	
	1-57071-164-X	How to Buy a Condominium or Townhome	$16.95	
	1-57071-223-9	How to File Your Own Bankruptcy (4E)	$19.95	
	1-57071-224-7	How to File Your Own Divorce (3E)	$19.95	
	1-57071-227-1	How to Form Your Own Corporation (2E)	$19.95	
	1-57071-343-X	How to Form Your Own Partnership	$19.95	
	1-57071-228-X	How to Make Your Own Will	$12.95	
	1-57071-331-6	How to Negotiate Real Estate Contracts (3E)	$16.95	
	1-57071-332-4	How to Negotiate Real Estate Leases (3E)	$16.95	
	1-57071-225-5	How to Register Your Own Copyright (2E)	$19.95	
	1-57071-226-3	How to Register Your Own Trademark (2E)	$19.95	
	1-57071-349-9	How to Win Your Unemployment Compensation Claim	$19.95	
	1-57071-167-4	How to Write Your Own Living Will	$9.95	
	1-57071-344-8	How to Write Your Own Premarital Agreement (2E)	$19.95	
	1-57071-333-2	Jurors' Rights (2E)	$9.95	
	1-57248-032-7	Legal Malpractice and Other Claims against...	$18.95	
	1-57071-400-2	Legal Research Made Easy (2E)	$14.95	
	1-57071-336-7	Living Trusts and Simple Ways to Avoid Probate (2E)	$19.95	
	1-57071-345-6	Most Valuable Bus. Legal Forms You'll Ever Need (2E)	$19.95	
	1-57071-346-4	Most Valuable Corporate Forms You'll Ever Need (2E)	$24.95	
	1-57071-347-2	Most Valuable Personal Legal Forms You'll Ever Need	$14.95	
	0-913825-41-7	Neighbor vs. Neighbor	$12.95	
	1-57071-348-0	The Power of Attorney Handbook (3E)	$19.95	
	1-57248-020-3	Simple Ways to Protect Yourself from Lawsuits	$24.95	
	1-57071-337-5	Social Security Benefits Handbook (2E)	$14.95	
	1-57071-163-1	Software Law (w/diskette)	$29.95	
	0-913825-86-7	Successful Real Estate Brokerage Mgmt.	$19.95	
	1-57071-399-5	Unmarried Parents' Rights	$19.95	
	1-57071-354-5	U.S.A. Immigration Guide (3E)	$19.95	
	0-913825-82-4	Victims' Rights	$12.95	
	1-57071-165-8	Winning Your Personal Injury Claim	$19.95	
		CALIFORNIA TITLES		
	1-57071-360-X	CA Power of Attorney Handbook	$12.95	
	1-57071-355-3	How to File for Divorce in CA	$19.95	
	1-57071-356-1	How to Make a CA Will	$12.95	
	1-57071-408-8	How to Probate an Estate in CA	$19.95	
	1-57071-357-X	How to Start a Business in CA	$16.95	
	1-57071-358-8	How to Win in Small Claims Court in CA	$14.95	
	1-57071-359-6	Landlords' Rights and Duties in CA	$19.95	
		FLORIDA TITLES		
	1-57071-363-4	Florida Power of Attorney Handbook (2E)	$12.95	
	1-57071-403-7	How to File for Divorce in FL (5E)	$21.95	
	1-57071-401-0	How to Form a Partnership in FL	$19.95	
	1-57248-004-1	How to Form a Nonprofit Corp. in FL (3E)	$19.95	
	1-57071-380-4	How to Form a Corporation in FL (4E)	$19.95	
	1-57071-361-8	How to Make a FL Will (5E)	$12.95	
		Form Continued on Following Page	**SUBTOTAL**	

To order, call Sourcebooks at 1-800-43-BRIGHT or FAX (630)961-2168 (Bookstores, libraries, wholesalers—please call for discount)

SPHINX® PUBLISHING ORDER FORM

Qty	ISBN	Title	Retail	Ext.
		FLORIDA TITLES (CONT'D)		
_____	1-57248-056-4	How to Modify Your FL Divorce Judgement (3E)	$22.95	_____
_____	1-57071-364-2	How to Probate an Estate in FL (3E)	$24.95	_____
_____	1-57248-005-X	How to Start a Business in FL (4E)	$16.95	_____
_____	1-57071-362-6	How to Win in Small Claims Court in FL (6E)	$14.95	_____
_____	1-57071-335-9	Landlords' Rights and Duties in FL (7E)	$19.95	_____
_____	1-57071-334-0	Land Trusts in FL (5E)	$24.95	_____
_____	0-913825-73-5	Women's Legal Rights in FL	$19.95	_____
		GEORGIA TITLES		
_____	1-57071-387-1	How to File for Divorce in GA (3E)	$19.95	_____
_____	1-57248-047-5	How to Make a GA Will (2E)	$9.95	_____
_____	1-57248-026-2	How to Start and Run a GA Business (2E)	$18.95	_____
		ILLINOIS TITLES		
_____	1-57071-405-3	How to File for Divorce in IL (2E)	$19.95	_____
_____	1-57071-415-0	How to Make an IL Will (2E)	$12.95	_____
_____	1-57071-416-9	How to Start a Business in IL (2E)	$16.95	_____
		MASSACHUSETTS TITLES		
_____	1-57071-329-4	How to File for Divorce in MA (2E)	$19.95	_____
_____	1-57248-050-5	How to Make a MA Will	$9.95	_____
_____	1-57248-053-X	How to Probate an Estate in MA	$19.95	_____
_____	1-57248-054-8	How to Start a Business in MA	$16.95	_____
_____	1-57248-055-6	Landlords' Rights and Duties in MA	$19.95	_____
		MICHIGAN TITLES		
_____	1-57071-409-6	How to File for Divorce in MI (2E)	$19.95	_____
_____	1-57248-077-7	How to Make a MI Will (2E)	$12.95	_____
_____	1-57071-407-X	How to Start a Business in MI (2E)	$16.95	_____
		MINNESOTA TITLES		
_____	1-57248-039-4	How to File for Divorce in MN	$19.95	_____
_____	1-57248-040-8	How to Form a Simple Corporation in MN	$19.95	_____
_____	1-57248-037-8	How to Make a MN Will	$9.95	_____
_____	1-57248-038-6	How to Start a Business in MN	$16.95	_____

Qty	ISBN	Title	Retail	Ext.
		NEW YORK TITLES		
_____	1-57071-184-4	How to File for Divorce in NY	$19.95	_____
_____	1-57071-183-6	How to Make a NY Will	$12.95	_____
_____	1-57071-185-2	How to Start a Business in NY	$16.95	_____
_____	1-57071-187-9	How to Win in Small Claims Court in NY	$14.95	_____
_____	1-57071-186-0	Landlords' Rights and Duties in NY	$19.95	_____
_____	1-57071-188-7	New York Power of Attorney Handbook	$19.95	_____
		NORTH CAROLINA TITLES		
_____	1-57071-326-X	How to File for Divorce in NC (2E)	$19.95	_____
_____	1-57071-327-8	How to Make a NC Will (2E)	$12.95	_____
_____	0-913825-93-X	How to Start a Business in NC	$16.95	_____
		PENNSYLVANIA TITLES		
_____	1-57071-177-1	How to File for Divorce in PA	$19.95	_____
_____	1-57071-176-3	How to Make a PA Will	$12.95	_____
_____	1-57071-178-X	How to Start a Business in PA	$16.95	_____
_____	1-57071-179-8	Landlords' Rights and Duties in PA	$19.95	_____
		TEXAS TITLES		
_____	1-57071-330-8	How to File for Divorce in TX (2E)	$19.95	_____
_____	1-57248-009-2	How to Form a Simple Corporation in TX	$19.95	_____
_____	1-57071-417-7	How to Make a TX Will (2E)	$12.95	_____
_____	1-57071-418-5	How to Probate an Estate in TX (2E)	$19.95	_____
_____	1-57071-365-0	How to Start a Business in TX (2E)	$16.95	_____
_____	1-57248-012-2	How to Win in Small Claims Court in TX	$14.95	_____
_____	1-57248-011-4	Landlords' Rights and Duties in TX	$19.95	_____

SUBTOTAL THIS PAGE _____

SUBTOTAL PREVIOUS PAGE _____

Illinois residents add 6.75% sales tax
Florida residents add 6% state sales tax plus applicable discretionary surtax _____

Shipping— $4.00 for 1st book, $1.00 each additional _____

TOTAL _____

DATE			